THE WORLD'S
GREATEST

TRIALS

THE WORLD'S GREATEST

TRIALS

BY
TIM HEALEY

OCTOPUS BOOKS

First Published 1986
by Octopus Books Ltd
59 Grosvenor St
London W1

© 1986 Octopus Books Limited

ISBN 0 7064 2498 0

Printed in Great Britain by
Richard Clay (The Chaucer Press) Ltd,
Bungay, Suffolk

Contents

CHAPTER 1: **A Question of Murder** _____6

CHAPTER 2: **Enemies of the State** _____33

CHAPTER 3: **Curious Cases** _____60

CHAPTER 4: **Matters of Public Concern** ___73

CHAPTER 5: **Society Scandals** _____92

CHAPTER 6: **Shadows of War** _____122

CHAPTER 7: **Historic Precedents** _____146

Introduction

Murder, treason and scandal! The courtrooms of the world have provided stage-settings for some of the most gripping human dramas of all time.

Lovers, poisoners, mothers, maniacs, peers, prostitutes, spies, labourers, terrorists, crusaders, war criminals, charmers, cheats . . . a fantastic pageant of human types has filed into history's dock.

In hanging days, great trials might be life or death matters which ended in horror on the scaffold. Today, a jury's verdict may still make the difference between triumphant release and a lifetime endured behind bars.

The evidence may be slight: a smudged fingerprint, say, or some suspicious remark to a witness. But even such delicate weights have been known to tilt the scales of justice. Small wonder that mystery still lingers about some of the most famous cases: mystery and its nagging sidekick, reasonable doubt.

CHAPTER 1

A Question of Murder

Lindy Chamberlain	Ronald True
Mrs Maybrick	Dr Crippen
Sacco and Vanzetti	Leopold and Loeb
Madame Fahmy	Peter Sutcliffe

'A dingo has got my baby!' LINDY CHAMBERLAIN

Shortly before nightfall on the evening of 17 August 1980, a group of campers were enjoying a barbecue near Ayers Rock in the Australian outback. Suddenly there was a shout.

'A dingo has got my baby!' called Mrs Lindy Chamberlain. In horror, her husband and other campers ran back to the Chamberlains' tent to find the baby girl's basket empty. 'All I could see was a horrible, lonely whiteness in that basket,' the father told police some time later. But other witnesses remembered traces of blood around the tent. And about a week later, the child's torn and bloodstained jumpsuit, singlet and nappy were found near the base of Ayers Rock. Of nine-week-old Azaria Chamberlain, however, there was no trace. She had vanished, never to be seen again.

It seemed a horrific tragedy, made all the more nightmarish by the looming presence of Ayers Rock — one of the weirdest things on planet earth. The vast red platform rises abruptly to more than 1,000 feet above the outback of the Northern Territory, forming the largest monolith in the world. Chameleon-like, its colour changes according to atmospheric conditions and the sun's position. The Aborigines have always regarded it as a magical place and the site of many strange happenings.

The baby's mysterious disappearance prompted a flood of gossip and speculation. Lindy and Michael Chamberlain, both in their thirties, were members of the Seventh Day Adventist Church, he being a minister. It was rumoured that the baby's name, Azaria, meant 'sacrifice in the wilderness'; had the little girl really been taken by a wild dog? How was it that the clothing had been found, while the baby's body had completely vanished? Many people came to regard the circumstances as suspicious, and the case won nationwide attention.

In February 1981 the coroner at Alice Springs delivered his verdict on the missing child. Taking the unprecedented step of reading his finding (a 13-page document) before television cameras, he informed an estimated viewing audience of two million people that the parents were entirely blameless. Azaria Chantal Loren Chamberlain had met her death while being attacked by a wild dingo; in trying to make off with the baby, 'the dingo would have caused severe crushing to the base of the skull and neck and lacerations to the throat and neck'. The body had been disposed of by a person or persons unknown, and neither the parents nor their sons Aidan (7) and Reagan (4), who had been camping with them at the time, were in any degree responsible. Moreover, 'I find that the name Azaria does not mean and never has meant "sacrifice in the wilderness." '

The coroner expressed sympathy for the bereaved parents: 'You have not only suffered the loss of your beloved child in the most tragic circumstances, but you have all been subjected to months of innuendoes, suspicion and probably the most malicious gossip ever witnessed in this country.' He declared that he had permitted TV coverage to stop the rumours in the most direct way possible.

It was a very emphatic performance — but the case simply would not die. A year later, in February 1982, a second inquest was called on the basis of new forensic evidence. On this occasion a forensic expert testified that traces of blood had been found on the clasp of a camera bag belonging to the parents. It was foetal blood — that is, the blood of a baby less than six months old — and with it was found baby hair. Blood had also been cleaned from conspicuous areas in the couple's car, but it had not been eradicated completely: there were traces in all sorts of nooks and crannies such as the door handles, the door hinge and places under the dashboard. The evidence was consistent with what was to become the prosecution's extraordinary allegation — that Mrs Chamberlain had taken the baby from the tent to the front seat of the car and there cut her throat. Afterwards, it was alleged, the body had been buried at the camp site, but dug up again. Azaria's clothing had been removed and placed at the spot where it was found several days later.

The coroner decided that there was a case for Mrs Chamberlain being sent to trial for murder, and her husband as an accessory in seeking to cover the act up. The accused parents were clearly stunned by the finding, and Michael Chamberlain remained for some time with his head buried in his hands, visibly distressed.

The 'Dingo Case' had now acquired a worldwide audience, and Lindy Chamberlain went into hiding before the trial. When proceedings opened on Monday 13 September, the world learned of a new twist in the drama. Mrs Chamberlain, 34, was seven months' pregnant — she might well give birth to another child during the trial.

The Supreme Court at Darwin was packed. So great was foreign interest that a separate room had to be set aside for the news media, with its own closed-circuit TV system linking up with proceedings in the court. The judge warned the jury not to allow anything they might have read to prejudice their verdict, while acknowledging that the publicity was 'without precedent in our lifetime'.

Mr Ian Barker QC, opening for the prosecution, said the foetal blood found in the car exploded the dingo story, which was no more than a 'fanciful lie to conceal the truth'. The prosecution would not try to establish Mrs Chamberlain's motive. But the evidence, he said, pointed conclusively to the fact that she had murdered her baby, entering the tent afterwards to leave the smears of blood that were found there later. The body was probably placed in the camera bag in the car prior to its eventual disposal.

In the weeks that followed, powerful evidence was marshalled to support the case. For example, Professor Malcolm Chaikin, head of textile technology at New South Wales University, declared that the baby's clothing had not been torn by a dingo's teeth but cut with some fairly sharp scissors; moreover, he claimed to have found some fragments of the material in Mrs Chamberlain's camera bag. James Malcolm Cameron, professor of forensic medicine, was flown in from the London Hospital medical college and also denied the likelihood of a wild dog's involvement. Asked what the clothing evidence pointed to, he said, 'It suggests that there was an incised wound of the neck. In other words, a cut throat.' The wound was caused by 'a cutting instrument across or around the neck held by a human element'.

The human story which emerged from campsite witnesses was, however, generally favourable to the defence. A Mrs Lowe was asked if anything in Lindy's behaviour prior to the disappearance had suggested that murder was on her mind. 'No, exactly the opposite,' replied the woman. 'She had a "new mum" glow about her.'

There was sobbing from the parents in the dock when another witness described how Lindy Chamberlain told her she had called her baby Azaria because it meant 'Blessed of God'.

Mrs Alice Amy Whittaker said she had seen a dingo emerging from

Lindy Chamberlain at the Alice Springs Court House

the bush while she was washing up at the camp site. It was skirting the lighted area and seemed to be moving towards the Chamberlains' tent. This was only 20 minutes before Michael Chamberlain rushed up to her and begged her and her husband to pray for Azaria because she had been taken by a dingo. Later that night Mrs Whittaker had comforted Lindy Chamberlain by saying that what had happened was God's will. Lindy tried to resign herself: 'It says, doesn't it, that at the Second Coming babies will be restored back to their mothers' arms?' But she was distressed and seemed particularly agitated by the idea that the searchers might be looking in the wrong place: 'I will have to live with this for the rest of my life. I don't want to have to if my baby simply died because I did not look in the right place.'

Some controversy surrounded the issue of dingoes' general habits. Was such an attack — with the removal of the prey — consistent with the wild dogs' known behaviour? Mr Leslie Harris, president of the Dingo Foundation, testified for the defence, asserting that a dingo might well regard a sleeping baby as prey and would be capable of carrying one off. A dingo, he said, might close its jaws over the entire head and make off with it so as not to lose its meal to other dingoes.

Several other witnesses testified to dingo attacks in the Ayers Rock area. One man described how his four-year-old son had been attacked by a wild dog at the same camp site only a month before Azaria's disappearance.

What of the bloodstains in the car? In June 1979 — a year before the event — the Chamberlains had picked up a man injured in a road accident. The victim testified in court that he had been bleeding profusely from the head. Of course, his was not foetal blood, but the damning evidence on this issue was challenged by the defence's own forensic witness, who claimed that the foetal blood test results were not reliable.

At one stage, the whole court travelled 800 miles to study the scene of the disappearance. Lindy Chamberlain was permitted to stay in Darwin, for she was by now eight months' pregnant. But she did give evidence when the court returned, in the fifth week of the trial.

Her version of events was already embodied in a statement made to police. She claimed that she had put Azaria to bed while her husband was at the barbecue, and afterwards came back to the cooking place to prepare a meal for her oldest son, Aidan. A baby's cry was heard from somewhere near the tent, and Lindy went back to check that all was well. As she walked towards the tent she saw a youngish dingo coming out of it; she yelled and briefly gave chase. Then, thinking only that her baby might have been bitten, she hurried into the tent.

In the box, Lindy Chamberlain was often emotional. She broke down in tears when asked to examine her baby's bloodstained clothing. When the judge asked if she was all right she said that she was — but two of the three women on the jury began crying and the trial had to be temporarily adjourned.

Lindy Chamberlain wept again that day when the prosecution's allegations were repeated; 'It's not true,' she declared through stifled sobs. The next day she broke down again, complaining to the prosecutor that 'you are talking about my baby, not some object.' And when it was alleged that she deliberately smeared the family tent with blood, she replied fiercely, 'No, that's pure fabrication.'

Summing up for the defence, her counsel asserted that there was no conceivable motive for the killing. Ten independent witnesses had been brought forward to testify that Lindy was a loving and caring mother to Azaria. The prosecution's whole story would be 'laughable if it was not such a horribly serious matter'.

What was the jury to make of it all? From the press reports, the forensic evidence did not appear conclusive either way, while the problem of motive was tormenting. Why should Lindy Chamberlain murder her baby? Was there anything in the rumour of a sacrifice? Or had she suffered from post-natal depression? Then again, if she was innocent, what on earth had happened to the body? Why were no bones or other human relics found? The fact of the matter was that, to many outsiders, the dingo and murder stories seemed improbable.

The jury of nine men and three women had, however, observed all the long and complex proceedings. And on Friday, 29 October, after deliberating for six hours, they returned unanimous verdicts of guilty: Lindy Chamberlain of murdering her baby and Michael Chamberlain of being an accessory after the fact. The trial judge, Mr Justice James Muirhead, passed the mandatory sentence of life imprisonment with hard labour on the convicted woman.

She received the sentence impassively, but was tearstained when driven from the court to Berrimah Prison on the outskirts of Darwin. Her husband, subsequently given an 18-month suspended sentence, was released on a promise of good behaviour, and immediately attended a church service with his sons.

A verdict had been reached on the missing baby — but what of the one to be born? On 17 November, under guard at a Darwin hospital, Lindy Chamberlain gave birth to a second girl. But she was not permitted to keep the child in prison, and Kahlia, as the baby was called, was taken from her mother only hours after the delivery. Australian justice was not so cruel, though, as to enforce a permanent separation. Two days later, Lindy Chamberlain was freed on bail pending an appeal; out of concern for the baby's welfare the mother was permitted to retire to an Adventist Church college with her family while awaiting the Appeal Court's ruling.

The judgement came in April 1983, when the Chamberlains' joint appeals were dismissed by the Federal Court in Sydney. The judges referred to the importance of seeing and hearing scientific witnesses in order to evaluate their testimony. As for the couple's credibility: 'If the jury disbelieved them, as they must have done, we are quite unable to say that they were wrong.'

Lindy Chamberlain was returned to jail, and all attempts to obtain her release failed until sensational new forensic evidence, including a baby's jacket, was found at Ayers Rock in January 1986. Yet another inquiry was ordered: Lindy Chamberlain was freed pending its outcome – and officials declared that whatever the result she would not be sent back to jail.

The mad major — a true story RONALD TRUE

Five blows with a rolling pin ended the life of 25-year-old prostitute Olive Young. She was bludgeoned to death in her basement flat in Fulham by a man who called himself Major True, and to make sure, the murderer thrust a towel down her throat and strangled her with the girdle of her dressing gown. Then True dragged the corpse into the bathroom and left it lying on the floor. He took his time, arranging a couple of pillows in the bed to make it look as though someone was asleep. Methodically, he went through the woman's possessions, taking £8 along with the best of her jewellery. And he was still there when the prostitute's cleaning lady arrived. He told her not to wake her mistress, and tipped her half a crown before leaving the flat.

The events had unfolded on the morning of 6 March 1922, and later that day True bought a new suit to replace the one bloodstained in the assault. He also pawned some of the stolen jewellery. All were acts of a cold and calculating murderer, you might think, of a man sufficiently in control of himself to both cover up and to profit from his crime. But the 'Major' had been recognized by the cleaning lady from an earlier visit, and was tracked down that night at the Hammersmith Palace of Varieties. Though he denied all knowledge of the murder, he was arrested and taken to Brixton Prison. He was not held there in the ordinary cells, however, but taken to the prison hospital. For the police and everyone else concerned with the case could see that True was stark, staring mad.

He really was mad: when the case came to trial at the Old Bailey the prosecution scarcely bothered to deny it, for the medical evidence was overwhelming and conclusive. But that did not mean that the defence could automatically expect an acquittal on grounds of insanity. It was to be a classic test for the rules governing crime and madness under the law of the land.

From his childhood, Ronald True had always been thought odd, and when he grew to manhood he became addicted to morphine, which cannot have helped his mental balance. But his strangeness worsened dramatically after accidents sustained as a trainee pilot in World War I. True never flew in combat for the Royal Flying Corps: he suffered a bad crash at Farnborough which resulted in concussion and left him unconscious for two days. After a second, less serious, accident at Gosport he was invalided out of the Corps.

From 1916 onwards, Ronald True lived his life in and out of nursing homes, where he alternated between fits of speechless gloom, of violence, and of wild exultation when he might, for example, speed around in his bath chair clutching a hooter and a doll. Around 1920 he also started to develop a persistent and sinister delusion. At a nursing home run by a Dr Parham, True used to place bets on horse races, receiving results by telegram. He was happy enough when he picked a winner, but when he lost he would complain that the result was not for him — it was for 'the other Ronald True'.

As time passed, 'the other Ronald True' came to take the blame for everything awkward and unpleasant such as unpaid bills and cheques that bounced. There would come a day of reckoning, True warned, if he ever caught up with his villainous double. There would be a fine 'how d'ye do'.

Outside the nursing homes, True was capable of seeming sane and agreeable — even rather good company — to passing acquaintances. The war had, after all, left a lot of decent young men prone to the horrors; to bouts of overanimated conversation and to sudden silences, and you could not blame True for such eccentricities as going about hatless, claiming that hats 'hurt his head'. He spoke of his wartime injuries. He posed as a 'Major' and fantasized about his exploits as a fighter ace in France. He claimed to be living a life of danger now, too, flying on secret and mysterious missions. To casual clubland friends all these things were acceptable as tallish stories. It was only on closer acquaintance that his lunacy became evident; his eyes, especially, were said to be terrifying.

Women in particular seem to have shunned him. For some time he pursued a Mrs Wilson, offering to act as her protector and scaring her out of her wits by threatening violence if she danced with other men. He showed Mrs Wilson his gun, too. Scotland Yard, he said, had given him permission to carry the revolver, loaded with dum-dum bullets, in case he should meet 'the other Ronald True' — a dangerous criminal who was going around the West End passing cheques which he, 'the real Ronald True', had to keep paying. Mrs Wilson tried her best to escape the lunatic's attentions, and finally freed herself from him in February 1922.

That was when Ronald True started pursuing the ill-fated prostitute Olive Young, alias Gertrude Yates. After an early and sinister encounter, she, like Mrs Wilson, perceived his derangement and tried to have nothing to do with him. But he was relentless in pursuit, phoning incessantly and trying to arrange meetings. True was also falling into debt, and signals seem to have got crossed in his brain. His shadow self and the woman who shunned him seem to have fused into one. For two weeks before the night of the murder, True was telling his acquaintances that he would shortly be going to a basement flat in Fulham to shoot a man who owed him money.

Late on the night of 5 March 1922, he was waiting on Olive Young's doorstep. Exhausted no doubt by his persecutions, and anxious to avoid a scene, she finally let the murderer in. . . .

When his case came to trial, the defence had no trouble in producing evidence of True's insanity. Even in prison he had exhibited his crazy cunning, managing to escape from his own cell and attain that of another killer with the declared intention of forming a Murderers' Club. But the prosecution looked coldly at the case in relation to the law. Here was a man in debt, who murdered a prostitute for her money and took some trouble to conceal the event afterwards. Mad or not, he *knew* what he was doing. And under the M'Naghten Rules (see page 149), that prohibited a plea of insanity.

The judge summed up in favour of the prosecution on the point of law: 'You will probably feel that the prisoner *did* know at the time the physical nature and quality of the acts he had perpetrated.' On 5 May 1922, Ronald True was found guilty of murder and sentenced to death.

Inevitably, there was an appeal — but the Appeal Court found no reason to disagree with the jury's verdict, and responsibility for his case rested finally with the Home Secretary, who ordered a commission to examine True's mental condition. Three doctors unanimously agreed that the prisoner was insane.

It was the doctors' decision at this stage which saved True's life. For it was a paradox of English law at the time of capital punishment that you could not hang a lunatic — you might sentence him or her to death, but the idea of executing mad creatures had been considered an abomination since Tudor times and before. For one thing the insane were not in a position to raise valid legal objections; for another, they could not make their peace with the Almighty.

And so Ronald True was reprieved and committed to Broadmoor. He died there in 1951, at the age of 60.

The arsenic-eater's wife MRS MAYBRICK

In 1884 an extraordinary murder case was reported from Liverpool. Two women, Mrs Flanagan and Mrs Higgins, confessed to killing Mr Higgins by poison which they had obtained by soaking arsenic out of flypapers. Since the women came from the working class, the case never quite became a classic. But only five years later another flypaper poison drama hit the headlines in Liverpool, and this one unfolded in a comfortable middle-class setting. Moreover, it featured a delicious cocktail of arsenic mixed with adultery—and culminated in one of the most controversial trial verdicts ever reached in an English court. The Maybrick Mystery was one of the grand Victorian crime blockbusters, and more than 30 years after the trial the name of the leading lady was still well remembered. When James Joyce wrote his novel *Ulysses* (1922) he had Molly soliloquize at length about the case in a passage beginning: 'take that Mrs Maybrick that poisoned her husband . . . white Arsenic she put in his tea off flypaper . . .' but did she?

Born Florence Elizabeth Chandler, the future Mrs Maybrick was a Southern belle from Mobile, Alabama, who was educated partly in Europe. In 1881, at the age of only 18, she married James Maybrick, a wealthy English cotton broker of 42. Three years later the couple settled down at Battlecrease House in Liverpool, where Mrs Maybrick bore her husband two children, a boy and a girl. And their family life seems to have been happy enough until, in 1887, Florence discovered that her husband had a mistress in Liverpool. James had sired no fewer than five children by the woman — two of them since his wedding.

It is clear that, afterwards, something froze between Mr and Mrs Maybrick. While keeping up outward appearances, they stopped sleeping together as man and wife. Increasingly, Florence looked for pleasure in the company of Alfred Brierley, a handsome young friend of her husband, while James continued to visit his mistress and indulge his favourite pastime — of eating arsenic.

It may sound incredible, but the people of Styria and the Tyrol had long practised arsenic-eating for therapeutic purposes; James Maybrick was a hypochondriac who took the substance both as a tonic and as an aphrodisiac. The Victorians were more cavalier with their medicines than we are today, and Maybrick also took a host of other potentially lethal preparations, including strychnine. But arsenic seems to have been his favourite. 'It is meat and liquor to me,' he once told a friend. 'I don't tell everybody. I take it when I can get it, but the doctors won't put any into my medicine except now and then. That only tantalizes me.' To another acquaintance he confided as he added some grey powder to a dish of food, 'You would be horrified, I dare say, if you knew what this is — it is arsenic. We all take some poison more or less. For instance, I am now taking arsenic enough to kill you.'

Mrs Maybrick knew something of her husband's addiction to medicines, and in March of 1889 she mentioned to the family doctor that James sometimes took a white powder which she thought might be strychnine. What was the likely result? The doctor replied that her husband ought to take care, because he could die. Then he joked, 'Well, if he should ever die suddenly, call me, and I can say you have had some conversation with me about it.'

Not long after this exchange, Mrs Maybrick for the first time spent an illicit weekend in London with Brierley. Her husband grew suspicious and on 29 March the Maybricks were seen quarrelling openly at the Grand National. There was a furious row at home, too, that evening, in which Maybrick beat his wife and dragged her around the bedroom. The following day, when the doctor treated her black eye, Mrs Maybrick told him that she intended to seek a separation.

Mrs Maybrick did not, in fact, open legal proceedings. But the row simmered on through April, and it was at the end of the month that Florence made a soon-to-be-notorious trip to a local chemist, where she bought a dozen arsenic-coated flypapers. Soon afterwards, the papers were seen by servants to be soaking in a washstand in Mrs Maybrick's bedroom.

On 25 April, James Maybrick drew up a new will leaving almost everything in trust for his children — and almost nothing to Florence.

On 28 April, James Maybrick was taken violently sick after eating a lunch that his wife had prepared for him. It was not the first time he had felt unwell — he had long suffered from dyspepsia, and complained of headaches and stiffness of the limbs. But that night he was dazed, vomiting, and practically numb in the legs. He recovered somewhat the next day, but in the week that followed he relapsed repeatedly. During this period Mrs Maybrick visited another local chemist — and bought another two dozen flypapers.

On 7 May, Maybrick collapsed, vomiting so severely that he could keep practically no food down. His tongue was badly furred and he experienced the tormenting and persistent sensation that he had a hair in his throat. The servants had never much liked Florence, and neither had Maybrick's family; nor had the flypaper poisonings of Mrs Flanagan and Mrs Higgins been forgotten in Liverpool. It was Alice Yapp, the children's nurse, who first voiced her suspicions, declaring to a family friend, 'Thank God, Mrs Briggs, you have come, for the mistress is poisoning the master.'

Was she? None of the doctors concerned with the case had suspected poisoning before; but now nurses, family and servants all started watching Mrs Maybrick with keen interest. And one evening, Florence was seen furtively removing a bottle of meat juice from the sick man's bedroom table; equally furtively, she brought it back two minutes later. Had she tampered with the contents? The bottle was quietly removed by a doctor, pending chemical analysis.

On other occasions, curious fragments of conversation were overheard from the sick room. Once, for example, Mrs Maybrick tried to get her husband to take some medicine. Maybrick flatly refused and said, 'Don't give me the wrong medicine again.'

'What are you talking about?' Mrs Maybrick replied. 'You never had the wrong medicine.'

James Maybrick died at 8.40 pm on the evening of Saturday, 11 May. And almost immediately his brothers Edwin and Michael locked Florence up while a search of the house was made. Hidden in a trunk in a linen cupboard was a packet labelled 'Arsenic — Poison for Cats'. Analysis confirmed that the bottle of meat juice, handled by Florence, had contained arsenic. And when arsenic was found in the dead man's stomach, Mrs Maybrick was formally arrested.

The trial opened on Wednesday, 31 July 1889 amid the most intense public interest. The press had got hold of all the key details and had effectively found the prisoner guilty already, so that the black van which conducted her to the Liverpool courthouse was booed and jeered by a vast crowd. Nevertheless, Mrs Maybrick — who wore black crêpe in the dock — replied with a clear 'Not guilty' when charged with murder, and the trial did not go entirely as the papers had anticipated.

The prosecutor's case was straightforward. He described the adulterous meeting with Brierley in London; the subsequent quarrel; the buying of flypapers and the sudden onset of the dead man's illness. There was the bottle of meat juice treated with arsenic, the packet of 'Arsenic — Poison for Cats'; a handkerchief had also been found soaked in arsenic, and arsenic was even found soaked into the pocket of a dressing gown worn by Mrs Maybrick. To cap it all, nurse Yapp had intercepted a letter written by Mrs Maybrick to Brierley, and this was read out at the trial. It had been composed during the early stages of Maybrick's illness, and to the Victorian court it was a thoroughly shocking document. While writing of her husband being 'sick unto death', Florence had seemed chiefly concerned to reassure her lover ('my own darling') that the details of their liaison were safe. Moreover, the doctors at that stage did not suspect that Maybrick's illness might be fatal — how did Florence know that he was 'sick unto death'?

But Mrs Maybrick was powerfully represented by a brilliant defence counsel in Sir Charles Russell, who had an answer for every suspicious circumstance. Take the famous flypapers, for example: Mrs Maybrick had from the moment of her arrest maintained that she bought and soaked these in order to prepare an arsenical face-wash to treat her complexion. Arsenic was in fact widely used in cosmetics at the time, and as Sir Charles pointed out, Mrs Maybrick bought the papers quite openly at shops where she was well known. Would she do so if she had any malign purpose? The papers were, moreover, left soaking all day for the servants to see.

The cosmetic face-wash explained the stained handkerchief and dressing-gown pocket. But what of the poisoned meat juice? Again, Mrs Maybrick had kept nothing back. She had candidly stated on arrest that throughout that particular evening her husband had been nagging her to give him one of the powders which he habitually took. She at first refused, but he begged her so piteously to put some in his food that in the end she agreed. But she had no idea that the substance concerned was arsenic — it was just one of James's 'powders'. As for the expression 'sick unto death' which had been used apparently prematurely, it was merely a Southern figure of speech meaning gravely — not necessarily fatally — ill.

Ultimately, the strength of the defence case lay in the medical evidence. Only a small quantity of arsenic was found in James Maybrick's stomach at the post mortem; there were traces of strychnine, hyoscine and morphine too. The hypochondriac had badly abused his stomach and had died from an acute inflammation which, the defence alleged, might have been provoked by almost anything. The distinguished Dr Tidy, one of the nation's leading forensic experts, testified for the defence and was quite unshakeable in his refusal to diagnose arsenic poisoning — or poisoning of any kind.

Prosecutor: He died from gastro-enteritis caused by an irritant?
Dr Tidy: Yes.
Prosecutor: It was some strong irritant, probably poison?
Dr Tidy: Some substance which to him acted as an irritant.
Prosecutor: Which was poisonous enough to kill him?
Dr Tidy: Which to him acted as an irritant.
Prosecutor: Can you suggest to us what it was?
Dr Tidy: No, I cannot.

This exchange continued for some time before the prosecutor retired defeated. The climax of the trial came when Mrs Maybrick herself was permitted, by the judge, to make a brief statement. (Under the law of the time, she was not allowed to give evidence and submit to questioning. Although this was changed in 1898 with the introduction of the Criminal Evidence Act.) Halting and tearful, she described how she prepared her arsenical face-wash; how she had mixed the powder into her husband's meat juice; and how, on the day before he died, she had fully confessed her adultery and received 'his entire forgiveness for the fearful wrong I had done him'.

Mrs Maybrick collapsed after speaking, and had to be revived with smelling salts. By now the court, the press and the public were all firmly on her side and an acquittal seemed almost certain. After all, it had not been conclusively proved that Maybrick died from arsenic at all — let alone that the prisoner had poisoned him. And if he *did* die of arsenic, it might well have been self-administered.

However, throughout the trial the judge, Mr Justice Stephen, had shown a certain lack of grip on the proceedings. He had recently suffered a stroke (and was soon to be admitted to an asylum) and in summing up he repeatedly blundered over the facts in a way detrimental to Mrs Maybrick's cause. To everyone's astonishment the jury found the prisoner guilty of murder, and while she sobbed and protested in the dock, sentence of death was passed upon her.

There was an immediate public outcry. The prosecution's witnesses were hissed and jostled as they left the court; nationwide petitions were raised; questions were asked in Parliament while, at the gaol where Mrs Maybrick was being held, flowers arrived by the cartload. In fact, Mrs Maybrick received several offers of marriage as the day of her execution drew nearer. Then, at the last minute, with her scaffold already built, the Home Secretary bowed to public pressure and commuted the sentence to life imprisonment.

Florence Maybrick served 15 years as a model prisoner before, in 1904, she was released. She went back to the United States, where she lectured for some time on the need for penal reform, always including her declaration, 'I swear to you I am innocent.' Eventually she disappeared from the public eye to live out her life as a recluse dependent chiefly on the charity of friends. She died in South Kent, Connecticut, in 1941 at the age of 76.

Did she do it? All who have studied the case agree that she should never have been convicted on the evidence. 'The element of doubt existed and it should have been resolved in her favour, because that is the law. . . . She was entitled to an acquittal,' wrote thriller-writer Raymond Chandler, a keen student of the case. He was fascinated not only by the mystery but by the coincidence that Mrs Maybrick's maiden name, Florence Chandler, was the same as his mother's. In fact, Chandler at one time planned a history of the affair, and took the trouble to itemize all the points for and against Mrs Maybrick's case.

What did the creator of private eye Philip Marlowe make of it all? 'I am pretty well convinced the dame was guilty,' Chandler wrote to a friend. But that was only one man's verdict — the fact is, nobody knows.

In the interests of science

In a Victorian poison trial as sensational as that of Mrs Maybrick, the ravishing young Adelaide Bartlett was tried at the Old Bailey in 1886 on the charge of murdering her husband Edwin with liquid chloroform.

The evidence was strongly against her. It was disclosed that her lover, a young Wesleyan minister named George Dyson, had bought quantities of chloroform for her shortly before the death, and a large amount of chloroform was found in the dead man's stomach. But how had it been administered? Edwin would not willingly have drunk it because of the searing pain it induced. Nor were there any corrosive traces in the mouth or windpipe.

Adelaide was acquitted, provoking the dry comment of surgeon Sir James Paget, 'Now that it is all over she should tell us, in the interests of science, how she did it.'

'This huge mass of flesh . . .' DR CRIPPEN

He is the most notorious domestic murderer in the annals of crime. Born in Michigan, Dr Hawley Harvey Crippen came to England in 1900. With him came his wife Cora, a failed opera singer and would-be music-hall artist who used the stage name of Belle Elmore. They were an outwardly respectable couple, though almost comically ill-matched: she was loud, ample-bosomed and domineering; he was small, balding and mild-mannered. Eventually the pair set up home at 39 Hilldrop Crescent, a semi-detached house in north London. And there, early in 1910, he murdered her.

Was there ever any doubt about it? Crippen's name has for so long been reviled that it is hard to imagine the time when his guilt was at all in question. But the case against him did not prove itself; some brilliant police and forensic work was required to prepare the evidence for a conviction. Spilsbury, who became an eminent forensic expert, contributed important evidence to this, his first famous case.

The last that any outsider saw of Belle Elmore was at a dinner party held by the Crippens on 31 January 1910. Afterwards, the little doctor informed his wife's friends that Belle had gone to America and died of a sudden illness there. He issued some suitably black-edged letters to that effect, and also moved his secretary and mistress, Ethel Le Neve, into Hilldrop Crescent, decking her out in Belle's jewellery and furs.

When the police asked questions about Belle's disappearance, Crippen changed his story and confided to them that his wife had really run away with another man. Since a search of the house revealed nothing, the case might have rested there. But the police inquiries seem to have broken Crippen's nerve, for he fled to Antwerp with Ethel Le Neve and there, using assumed names, the couple boarded the ss *Montrose* for Quebec. Crippen posed as a 'Mr John Robinson', while Ethel — with hair cropped and wearing boy's clothing — was 'Master Robinson', his son.

When Crippen fled the country, the police searched Hilldrop Crescent again, and this time Chief Inspector Walter Dew discovered human remains buried under the cellar floor. Warrants were quickly issued for the fugitives' arrest, and police bills were posted at the ports. The ss *Montrose* was only two hours out of Antwerp before the captain began to suspect the 'Robinsons', father and son; they were squeezing one another's hand in a manner 'unnatural for two males'. Later identifying the couple as Crippen and Le Neve, the captain radioed reports back to London. It was the first time that wireless telegraphy was used in a murder hunt, and it lent a sensational dimension to what was already a case packed with drama. Even as Inspector Dew hastened after the *Montrose* in a faster vessel, the captain's reports about the fugitives were being printed in the *Daily Mail* for the benefit of an enthralled public. Readers learned, for example, that Le Neve's disguise was flawed, her trousers being 'very tight about the hips, and are split a bit down the back and secured with large safety pins'. They discovered too that the unsuspecting Crippen 'is now reading *The Four Just Men*, which is all about a murder in London and £1,000 reward'.

Overtaken by Inspector Dew, Crippen was arrested on board the *Montrose* on 31 July 1910. As he was taken into custody, he said, 'I am not sorry; the anxiety has been too much.' In his pocket was found what appeared to be a suicide note addressed to his mistress:

'I cannot stand the horrors I go through every night any longer and as I see nothing bright ahead and money has come to an end I have made up my mind to jump overboard tonight. I know I have spoilt your life but I hope someday you can learn to forgive me. With last words of love. Your H.'

It has often been said that Crippen's trial, which opened on 18 October 1910, at the Old Bailey, was a mere formality. But Crippen pleaded

Dr Crippen with Ethel Le Neve leaving the SS Montrose

not guilty, and throughout the proceedings remained calm, polite and quietly firm in protesting his innocence. Briefly, his defence was that his wife had always been 'rather hasty in her temper', but that from around 1904 things got worse. Belle was always finding fault and picking quarrels, and this, he discovered, was because she had struck up a liaison with an American music-hall artist named Bruce Miller. Depressed at first, Crippen had later pursued an affair with his secretary, Ethel Le Neve, and had found in her all the love and companionship he needed. What motive could he have for suddenly murdering his wife?

Crippen said that after the dinner party on 31 January, Belle had worked herself up into one of her rages, informed him that she was leaving him the next day, and told him to 'cover up the scandal in the best way you can'. And that is precisely what he did. He went to work the following morning and never saw Belle again, so to 'cover up the scandal' he invented the story about her going to America and dying there of sudden pneumonia. He then moved his mistress in with him quite openly. Only when the police called did it occur to him that Belle's disappearance might be construed in a sinister way. And since he had lied about her death he foolishly decided to flee. The rest just followed naturally: expecting to be arrested on arrival in Canada, he had faked the suicide note to enable him to jump ship and disappear for a while until everything had blown over.

The story was not entirely implausible. But it ignored the gruesome remains found in the cellar at Hilldrop Crescent. Whose were they if not Belle Elmore's? And who could have buried them there if not Crippen himself?

The result of the trial really would have been a foregone conclusion had the remains comprised the recognizable corpse of Crippen's wife. But they did not. What Inspector Dew discovered under the cellar at Hilldrop Crescent was a makeshift grave where, buried in lime, was a mass of boneless flesh:

'The remains were what might be called close packed, heavily packed, with clay above them to a depth of 5 inches.'

'They were rammed in?' asked the prosecuting counsel.

'Yes, rammed in,' replied the inspector.

'Mixed up and folded over in parts, jumbled up all together?'

'All together; this huge mass of flesh was all together.'

The head, skeleton and limbs of Mrs Crippen were never found. A human heart, liver, lungs and kidneys were all present — but not the genitals, so that it was impossible to determine the sex of the victim. Crippen's counsel produced an expert to testify that flesh and organs can survive in an excellent state of preservation when buried in clay and quicklime. In short, the thrust of the defence was that the remains, 'whosesoever they were and whoever had buried them', could have been there for years; been buried there before the Crippens moved into the house in 1905.

And that was where Crippen's case collapsed. The prosecution showed that on 17 January Crippen bought from a chemist five grains of the potentially lethal drug hyoscine; chemical analysis demonstrated that a fatal dose of hyoscine was present in the remains. A piece of abdominal scar tissue was recovered and identified as the mark of an operation sustained by Mrs Crippen some years before. Also found was a woman's hair curler with a lock of dyed blonde hair in it — and Mrs Crippen dyed her hair blonde. But the clinching detail was a piece of a man's pyjama jacket in which remains had been wrapped; this, it was shown, had been bought by Crippen from Jones Brothers of Holloway as recently as January 1909.

Crippen's case sank under the weight of that 'huge mass of flesh' and what could be deduced from it. And it provided a macabre counterpoint to the romantic comedy of his flight in disguise with Le Neve. You had to picture the quiet, rather kindly little man poisoning his wife, then patiently dissecting the corpse; disposing of such durable items as head, hands and feet; burying the flesh; and tidying up before inviting his mistress, the shy typist Ethel Le Neve, to come and live on those same premises.

In a separate trial, Ethel Le Neve was acquitted of being an accessory. But Dr Hawley Harvey Crippen was found guilty of murder, and on 23 November 1910 was hanged at Pentonville.

'The last moment belongs to us . . .'

SACCO AND VANZETTI

On 15 April 1920, a paymaster and guard were killed during a payroll hold-up outside a shoe factory near Boston, Massachusetts. The bandits escaped, but three weeks later a pair of Italian immigrants were arrested on firearms charges and subsequently charged with the payroll murders. They were Nicola Sacco, a shoemaker, and Bartolomeo Vanzetti, a fish peddler — and their names were to echo through the decades to the shame of American justice.

The events occurred during one of America's periodic 'Red scares'. Sacco and Vanzetti held anarchist views, and their trial in May 1921 proved a grotesque travesty. The mere facts that the accused were immigrants and anarchists were practically enough to convict them, and their fates were sealed when the prosecution tried to prove by dubious means that Sacco's .32 Colt was the murder weapon. The prejudicial atmosphere of the court was barely credible: the accused were freely referred to as 'wops', 'dagos', and 'sons of bitches', and Judge Webster Thayer, in summing up, disclosed an open detestation of foreigners ('Did you see what I did to those anarchistic bastards?' he asked after the proceedings).

Sacco and Vanzetti were found guilty of first degree murder, but the courtroom charade had not passed unnoticed among American liberals. The immigrants' case became a *cause célèbre*, and through the next six years a campaign for retrial gathered ground on both sides of the Atlantic. Worldwide protests and mass fund-raising meetings contributed to various appeals, and the whole affair was complicated in 1925 when a convicted gangster, Celestino Madeiros, confessed to the payroll robbery and stated that Sacco and Vanzetti played no part in it. Since Madeiros himself was awaiting execution, however, his testimony was of limited value.

In July 1927, a three-man committee was appointed to re-examine the evidence. Authoritative new testimony for the prosecution came from Major Calvin Goddard, a pioneer of forensic ballistics. Using the recent invention of the comparison microscope, he showed conclusively that the fatal bullets *had* allegedly been fired by Sacco's gun (but had the bullets been planted on him? So much was at stake by now in the case that both defence and prosecution were fighting dirty).

On 3 August the state Governor refused a retrial. Sacco and Vanzetti must die, and following the final denial of clemency, riot squads were called out in several US cities, while bombs went off in New York and Philadelphia and there were strikes and riots in Europe and South America. It was all to no avail. Sacco and Vanzetti went to the electric chair in Boston's Charlestown Prison on 23 August 1927. Both men maintained their innocence to the end, and their deaths inspired a wealth of poems, novels and plays. If historians still raise some question marks over their innocence, it is certain that they should never have been convicted on the evidence: in 1977, a special proclamation by the Governor of Massachusetts officially cleared their names.

The most moving tribute to their memory, though, was penned by Vanzetti himself. In a statement written before his death he willingly accepted his martyrdom. He wrote of his pride that the pair of them — a shoemaker and a poor fish peddler — should have contributed by chance to such an upheaval in the public conscience: 'Never in our full life could we hope to do such work for tolerance, for justice, for man's understanding of men as now we do by accident. . . . The last moment belongs to us — that agony is our triumph.'

Murder for kicks

LEOPOLD AND LOEB

Richard Loeb and Nathan Leopold were members of wealthy Chicago families: 18-year-old Loeb was the son of the Vice President of Sears, Roebuck and Company, giants in the field of mail-order merchandise, while Leopold, 19, came from a similarly prosperous background. Both were intelligent; neither needed the money. Yet on 21 May 1924 they committed a stupid and brutal murder. The ostensible motive was $10,000 ransom — the truth was they did it for kicks.

The two youths enjoyed a weird relationship. Both were admirers of Nietzsche's philosophy, which taught that some people are supermen, not to be shackled by conventional morality. The suave Richard Loeb considered himself one of this elect, and the shorter, weak-sighted Nathan Leopold was happy to describe himself as his friend's slave.

It was Loeb who conceived the idea of the murder: a 'perfect crime' without motive, committed for the thrill of breaking the ultimate taboo. The ransom arrangements would all be invented to throw the authorities off the scent.

Fourteen-year-old Bobby Franks, son of a millionaire Chicago businessman, became their victim. The killers invited him into a car, which Leopold drove while Loeb clubbed the boy to death. The naked body was subsequently hidden in a culvert on some waste ground near a railway line, and acid was poured over the face to make it unidentifiable.

Afterwards, the killers telephoned the boy's mother, posing as kidnappers, and sent a typewritten ransom note signed 'GEORGE JOHNSON', giving instructions on how the money should be paid.

It turned out to be a far from perfect crime. The body was quickly discovered and identified without trouble, despite the disfiguring acid. Spectacles found near the scene were traced through oculists' records to Leopold, who offered a very weak story for their presence there. Then he was asked about his typewriter. The ransom note had been tapped out on an Underwood portable, and Leopold denied possessing such a machine. But it was soon discovered that he had loaned his typewriter to some fellow students. When located, it was identified as the machine which had typed the ransom note.

Meanwhile Loeb had made himself conspicuous during routine inquiries among wealthy Chicago families, by being over-talkative and 'helpful' about the murder inquiry. He was known to be a close friend of Leopold, and under persistent questioning, the superman broke down and fully confessed.

What more callous murder could possibly be committed? The case outraged public opinion in the United States, and there were loud calls for the death penalty to be applied. Indeed, it was expected that the two youths would be executed, until Clarence Darrow took on the case for the defence. A humanitarian and social reformer, the great Clarence Seward Darrow was passionately opposed to capital punishment. He was also a brilliant lawyer — so brilliant that during his entire career only one out of the 50-odd people he defended on charges of first degree murder was ever executed.

Darrow was basically a pessimist. 'We all know life is futile,' he once wrote. 'A man who considers that his life is of very wonderful importance is awfully close to a padded cell.' But out of that pessimism he drew strength: life might be futile, but people could through hope and reason invent a kind of sense for it.

The trial took place in July 1924. Darrow asked for mitigation on grounds of reduced responsibility and mental illness. How, he asked, could an act so bad *not* be mad? By what standards could the crime of Leopold and Loeb be described as the work of sane young men?

It is a paradox that has often been raised since in the cases of infamous murderers. But it carried no great legal weight; more to their advantage was the sheer youth of Darrow's clients. Teenage violence and juvenile delinquency were not yet familiar concepts, capable of hardening adult attitudes. Leopold and Loeb seemed so very young, with so much of their lives before them. In an impassioned speech which spanned two days, Darrow quoted freely from literature on the horror of youth meeting death on the scaffold. He quoted from Omar Khayyám and from A. E. Housman (or rather, in Housman's case he *mis*quoted, as the poet himself testily complained). And at the end of the sensational murder trial, his pleas saved the two young men. The judge passed sentences of life imprisonment for murder, with 99 years on the kidnapping charge.

Richard Loeb was killed in 1936, during a prison brawl. Nathan Leopold served 33 years of his sentence before, amid some controversy, he was paroled in 1958. He married and lived in Puerto Rico, dying in 1971, having written a book about his experiences.

Burke and Hare

In Edinburgh's sensational body-snatching trial of 1828, William Burke was tried and sentenced to death, while his equally notorious accomplice William Hare got off scot free for turning King's Evidence. The pair of them had murdered to provide bodies for an anatomist to dissect; Burke was hanged before a vast crowd in January 1829 and his corpse was handed over to the College of Surgeons — ironically, for purposes of dissection.

Death of a playboy prince MADAME FAHMY

The public in the 1920s was fascinated by the mysterious East: it was the decade when Valentino was *The Sheik* and Fairbanks was *The Thief of Baghdad*; when Tutankhamun's tomb was opened and when, throughout the Western world, crop-haired jazz girls daubed their eyelids with Egyptian kohl. And in 1923 there occurred a sensational murder trial to match the taste of the period. In a sumptuous suite at the Savoy Hotel, Madame Marie-Marguérite Fahmy shot dead her Egyptian playboy husband, Prince Ali Kamel Fahmy Bey. He had treated her, it seemed, like an Oriental beast. To the case's exotic mixture of sex, luxury and blood were added the talents of Sir Edward Marshall Hall, the most flamboyant defence counsel of the age. Small wonder that the Savoy Shooting stole the front-page headlines.

Madame Fahmy, the accused, was a glamorous Parisian brunette aged 32 at the time of the trial. The Prince, ten years younger, was a wealthy Egyptian and attaché at the French Legation in Cairo. The couple had met in Paris during May of 1922, at which time she was a divorcée. And she progressed quickly from becoming the Prince's mistress to becoming his wife; the pair were married in December of that year. Madame Fahmy accepted the Muslim faith for the purpose of the wedding, but insisted on her right to wear Western clothes. She also stipulated that she retain the right of divorce, but this was not acknowledged by her husband. Prince Fahmy considered his wife bound to him under Muslim law: he possessed the sole right of divorce (as well as the right to take three more wives should he wish to do so).

The marriage was disastrous. Whatever infatuation was present at the outset, the couple quarrelled wherever they lived as man and wife: in Paris, Cairo and in London, to which they came in July of 1923. Often Prince Fahmy beat his wife, once so severely that her jaw was dislocated. On another occasion he kept her locked up for three days on his yacht; on yet another he swore an oath on the Koran that one day he would kill her. This was done with such solemnity that the frightened woman wrote formally to her lawyer accusing her husband if she should ever disappear! 'Yesterday, January 21, 1923, at three o'clock in the afternoon, he took his Bible or Koran — I do not know how it is called — kissed it, put his hand on it, and swore to avenge himself upon me tomorrow, in eight days, a month, three months, but I must disappear by his hands. This oath was taken without any reason, neither jealousy, nor a scene on my part.' As for the Prince, he really does seem to have regarded his wife as a creature to be mastered by force. 'Just now I am engaged in training her,' he once wrote. 'With women one must be severe — no bad habits.'

They had been at the Savoy for barely a week when the fatal row broke out. On the evening of 9 July, the couple quarrelled violently in the hotel restaurant, and Madame Fahmy, it was to be said at the trial, shouted in French, 'You shut up. I will smash this bottle over your head.' Asked by the band leader if she wanted anything special played, she answered, 'I don't want any music — my husband has threatened to kill me tonight.' Upstairs, at about 1.30 am, the quarrel was still going on. A porter saw Prince Fahmy burst from his room in his pyjamas, a flushed mark on his cheek. 'Look at my face!' he fumed. 'Look what she has done!' Then Madame Fahmy came out too, still in her white, beaded evening dress, and shouted furiously in French.

The porter ushered them back into their suite, and walked on down the corridor. Moments later, three shots detonated. Rushing back to the suite, the porter saw Madame Fahmy toss down a .32 Browning automatic. The Prince lay bleeding from headwounds, and died not long after in hospital.

Charged with murder, Madame Fahmy was brought to trial at the Old Bailey in September 1923. Her cause inevitably stirred up a lot of public sympathy, but sympathy alone does not win court cases. Madame Fahmy had manifestly shot her husband dead at point-blank range in the heat of a domestic quarrel. And it would need all the talents of her defence counsel, Marshall Hall, to get her off the hook.

He gave the case everything he had got. Handsome, and flamboyant in style, the advocate was famed for theatrical effects which have disappeared from the modern lawyer's repertoire. But they still swayed juries in the 1920s, and Marshall Hall was their leading exponent.

Of course, he dwelled on Prince Fahmy's cruelty, cataloguing the beatings and humiliations endured by his wife. But there was more to be said against the dead man. Marshall Hall suggested that he was a homosexual who enjoyed a compromising relationship with his male secretary. Madame Fahmy, it was alleged, had been made to submit to a nameless but nauseating sexual indignity (presumably anal intercourse), and suffered painful illness in consequence. In fact, that illness was what provoked the quarrel on the fateful night. She had asked for money to pay for an operation in Paris, and he told her that she could only have it if she agreed to indulge his whim. 'I will if you do something for me,' he had said, before starting to tear off her dress.

When Madame Fahmy refused, he half strangled her. 'He seized me suddenly and brutally by the throat with his left hand,' she testified in French. (All of her statements were made in her native tongue and delivered to the court through an interpreter.) 'His thumb was on my windpipe and his fingers were pressing on my neck. I pushed him away but he crouched to spring on me, and said "I will kill you!" '

'I lifted my arm in front of me and without looking pulled the trigger. The next moment I saw him on the ground before me. I do not know how many times the revolver went off.' She had thought that the gun was empty of cartridges. 'I thought the sight of the pistol might frighten him,' she sobbed under cross-examination.

Marshall Hall's final speech to the jury was regarded as the most dramatic of his brilliant career. Having cast the Prince as an Oriental monster of depravity, he impersonated him, stalking across the court in emulation of his advance on his wife. Then, pistol in hand, the advocate took the part of his client: 'As he crouched for the last time, crouched like an animal, retired for the last time to get a bound forward — she turned the pistol and put it to his face.'

Suddenly, Marshall Hall levelled the gun at the foreman of the jury. He paused for a moment: 'And to her horror the thing went off!'

All eyes were fixed on the tableau. The court was in total silence. And then Marshall Hall released the gun, which clattered to the floor — exactly as Madame Fahmy had dropped it.

It was a spellbinding moment, and the advocate had further touches of courtroom magic in store. Concluding his address, he referred to the Oriental darkness into which the prisoner had been plunged by her marriage. 'I ask you to open the gate and let this Western woman go back into the light of God's great Western sun,' he ended, extending a prophetic arm high up to the Old Bailey skylight. A shaft of sun came through — right on cue.

In no time at all, the jury had found Madame Fahmy not guilty of murder; not guilty of manslaughter either. Such volcanic cheers erupted with the verdict that the judge ordered the public benches to be cleared and it was in an emptied court that Madame Fahmy sobbed her gratitude as she was released from custody, a free woman.

The whole case had become a triumph for 'Western light' over 'Oriental darkness' in an almost offensive manner. In fact, Marshall Hall received a formal complaint from the leader of the Egyptian Bar, accusing him of castigating all Egypt and indeed the entire East in order to save his client. The truth is that the fictional ideal of *The Sheik* had met a horribly flawed counterpart in Prince Fahmy. Marshall Hall had merely toyed with the conventions of his day, reversing the romantic image to make the dead playboy an archetype of evil.

> **Lizard Panic**
> Nairobi—Police in the city of Mombasa were looking for 20 suspects who escaped from a courtroom when a giant lizard entered the chambers, causing panic. Everybody, including guards, ran for safety.
> *The Times,* 3 OCTOBER 1984

Judgement on the Ripper PETER SUTCLIFFE

A notice, handwritten by Bradford lorry-driver Peter Sutcliffe, was displayed in the cab of his vehicle. It read:

> IN THIS TRUCK IS A MAN WHOSE LATENT GENIUS
> IF UNLEASHED WOULD ROCK THE NATION,
> WHOSE DYNAMIC ENERGY WOULD
> OVERPOWER THOSE AROUND HIM.
> BETTER LET HIM SLEEP?

The humour sours when you remember that Sutcliffe turned out to be the Yorkshire Ripper — a man who killed and horribly mutilated 13 women in his five-year reign of terror.

The murders began in October 1975 with the killing of Wilma McCann, a 28-year-old prostitute whose corpse, battered by hammer-blows to the skull and pierced by screwdriver stab-wounds, was discovered on a Leeds playing field. The Ripper's next three victims had all plied the same trade in the red light districts of Leeds and Bradford. But the pattern of murder changed in June 1977 when a perfectly respectable 16-year-old girl fell victim to the killer's brutal impulse. Other non-prostitutes were to succumb later; the case brought stark terror to the women of West Yorkshire, and indeed all over Britain.

It also prompted the biggest murder hunt of the century. But in January 1981, when the Ripper was finally caught, it happened almost by chance. The bearded Sutcliffe was discovered by Sheffield police in his Rover V8 with a coloured prostitute named Ava Reivers. The car carried false number plates, and contained the grim tools of the Ripper's trade: a hammer, garotte and sharpened Philips type screwdriver. Ava Reivers could count herself the luckiest woman in Britain that night — she would have been the next victim.

Back at the police station, the police knew that they had found the Ripper at last. He turned out to be a married man, born in 1946 at Bingley near Bradford and now living in a respectable middle-class district of that city. In his time he had held down a variety of jobs — including that of gravedigger at Bingley Cemetery. Ironically, he had been interviewed routinely no fewer than nine times before in the police trawl for the mystery killer.

What had motivated him? In August 1974, Sutcliffe had married a

Peter Sutcliffe on his wedding day

demure schoolteacher named Sonia Szurma; the murders started little more than a year later and many people speculated that, in killing his victims, Sutcliffe was really trying to destroy his wife. Though the couple seemed loving and were well liked, there were known to be rows. It was Sonia who did the shouting; the slightly built Sutcliffe would meekly ask only that she keep her voice down so as not to disturb the neighbours. Sonia had, moreover, suffered a period of mental illness in which she believed, among other things, that she was the Second Coming of Christ. In short, there were tensions in the household — tensions which hardly explain the Ripper's acts, but help to fill in their background.

The three-week trial took place at the Old Bailey in May 1981. Fascination with the case was international, and illegally taken photographs of Sutcliffe in the dock were published in foreign magazines. The trial also raised important questions about the way in which the Ripper case had been handled by police: the £4 million manhunt had been badly misled by a hoax tape sent by a man with a Geordie accent who had posed as the Ripper. But the overriding issue, on which Sutcliffe's fate depended, was whether he was mad or not.

Peter William Sutcliffe was charged with the murder of 13 women and attempts to kill another seven. He denied the murder charges — but admitted manslaughter on the grounds of diminished responsibility.

Under the 1957 Homicide Act, a prisoner may plead for a reduced charge of manslaughter on the grounds that he or she suffered some 'abnormality of mind' which impaired his or her mental responsibility. In the Ripper case, the Attorney General was prepared to accept such a plea. But the judge was unhappy that the murder charges should be so easily disposed of; he insisted that the case go before a jury. And so it was left to twelve ordinary people — six men, six women — to judge the killer's state of mind.

From a certain point of view, anyone who did what Sutcliffe did must be mad. But the law cannot accept such a proposition, for it would result in a legal absurdity. Every crime is an abnormal act, so anyone who committed one might claim 'abnormality of mind' in expectation of lenient treatment. Sutcliffe's defence was more specific: he alleged that he had heard voices ordering him to kill prostitutes; his had been a 'divine mission'. In prison, he had been examined by three psychiatrists who unanimously declared him to be a paranoid schizophrenic.

Impassive in the dock, Sutcliffe gave no clue as to his mental condition. But against the experts' testimony was the possibility that the prisoner had simply faked his symptoms. For example, he had not mentioned hearing voices until several interviews after his capture. In custody he was alleged to have remarked that if found to be 'loony' he would serve only 10 years instead of 30. From Sonia's bout of mental disturbance he could have recalled convincing symptoms such as tactile hallucinations (he claimed that he had experienced a hand tightening around his heart).

But perhaps the most damning flaw in his story was the simple fact that many of his victims were not prostitutes at all. There was teenage Jayne Macdonald, Josephine Whitaker, clerk in a building society, Barbara Leach and Jacqueline Hill, students, Margo Walls, a 47-year-old civil servant.

On 22 May 1981, the jury retired, deliberating for 5 hours and 55 minutes. On return, they found Peter William Sutcliffe guilty of murder. He was sentenced to life imprisonment, the judge recommending that a minimum of 30 years be served. In the streets outside the Old Bailey, when news of the verdict arrived, a large crowd gave three cheers for the jury. It was reported that even in the psychiatric community, relief was immense that the experts' testimony had been rejected.

Mystery, though, still surrounds the Ripper's mind. In prison at Parkhurst he continued to claim hearing voices, and in March 1984 the Home Secretary ordered his removal to Broadmoor. Peter Sutcliffe, he disclosed, was in a condition of grave mental illness, doctors both at Parkhurst and Broadmoor diagnosing paranoid schizophrenia. His state of mind had seriously deteriorated since admission to prison, and he could now be a threat to prison staff and others.

Was he mad all along? Or did he go mad faking madness?

CHAPTER 2

Enemies of the State

Gary Powers
Guy Fawkes
Alfred Dreyfus
Jiang Qing

Sir Walter Raleigh
Charles I
Marinus Van Der Lubbe

The spy who fell to earth GARY POWERS

In May 1960, a summit meeting was scheduled to take place in Paris between Dwight Eisenhower, US President, and Nikita Khrushchev, the Soviet premier. The conference was designed to ease Cold War tensions in a nervous world that was only just learning to live in the shadow of the atomic bomb. Much was expected of the talks — but they never took place. In a sensational propaganda coup, the Soviets announced that they had brought down an American U–2 spy plane which had been flying over Russian territory. How could the talks take place in the face of such imperialist treachery?

On the American side, every conceivable blunder was made. State Department officials immediately denied that any such flight had been made. The downed craft, said Washington, was a weather observation plane which had drifted by accident over the Soviet border. The announcement played right into Khrushchev's hands, for, having delayed the news, the premier now revealed that parts of the wrecked plane had been recovered, including high-altitude cameras, recording equipment and film of Soviet installations. To cap it all, the pilot, 31-year-old Kentucky-born Gary Powers, was in Soviet hands. *Weather craft? Drifted?*

Eisenhower was forced to come clean. In an unprecedented admission, he confessed that he had authorized high-altitude espionage flights over Russia. Vice-President Nixon even went on television to declare that they were part of US policy — and would continue.

Khrushchev had a field day, demanding that if the talks were to go ahead the President must apologize before the world, punish his guilty advisers and give assurances that such incursions would never be repeated. Eisenhower, horribly embarrassed by the whole affair, could not swallow these ultimate humiliations. He refused an apology — the Russians boycotted the talks — and the summit meeting collapsed.

It had been a moral triumph for Khrushchev, and all that remained to seal his victory was to stage the grand show trial of Gary Powers. It opened in Moscow's Hall of Columns on 17 August 1960, before batteries of TV cameras and the flashbulbs of countless pressmen. Though the proceedings were carried out in Russian, simultaneous translations were made available in English, French, German and Spanish. Let the whole world judge the majesty of Soviet justice!

In fact, the event was quite unlike the notorious show trials of Stalin's era. There was no need for the prisoner to be brainwashed; no need for the evidence to be fabricated. Francis Gary Powers had been caught fair and square on an illicit overflight — he had only to be led through his story.

Powers, it transpired, had been born in Bourdoyne, Kentucky, of a working-class family and volunteered for the Air Force in 1950. Two years later, towards the end of his period of military service, he was interviewed and recruited by the CIA for reconnaissance flights along the Soviet border. Given the cover name of 'Palmer', he was trained for 2½ months in Nevada in the handling of U–2 aircraft, which at the time represented the ultimate in aerial reconnaissance technology. Each incorporated a jet engine inside a glider frame, with a wingspan twice the length of the fuselage. Built by Lockheed, the U–2s were capable of flying at 68,000 feet, an altitude undreamed of before.

From 1956–60, Powers flew U–2s with a team of six other pilots along the frontier between Turkey and the Soviet Union. Although he had previously violated Soviet airspace, the fateful mission of 1 May 1960 was his first deep penetration of Soviet territory. He was briefed beforehand by a Colonel Shelton, and his route was to take him from Peshawar in West Pakistan across the very heartland of the Soviet Union, to end up at Bodö in Norway. At certain named locations on the route he was to turn on and off the control knobs of camera and recording equipment. . . .

'The Colonel also said that just in case anything should happen he was giving me some packages with Soviet money and some gold coins, which I might use to bribe Soviet citizens to help me, if I needed help. They were put into my flying suit pockets. He also had

Gary Powers holding a model of a U-2 plane

a silver dollar coin which he showed me which had a needle installed in it. He said that there was no danger because no USSR aircraft or rocket could get to my altitude, but in case something happened and I was captured, the needle contained poison and, if I was tortured and I could not stand it, I could use the needle to kill myself.'

Powers took off at 5 am and crossed the Soviet border only half an hour later. He was flying at the maximum 68,000 feet and (despite what the Colonel had told him) he was both tracked by, and within the range of, Soviet anti-aircraft systems. Four hours after take-off, as he was approaching Sverdlovsk, 'I saw, that is felt, a sort of hollow-sounding explosion. It seemed to be behind me. I could see an orange flash or an orange-coloured light behind me.'

When he realized he had been hit, Powers had to act quickly. The U–2 was equipped with a destructor switch which would give him 70 seconds to clear the aircraft by ejector seat. However, the ejector had jammed. The plane was spinning groundward and Powers only managed to escape by opening the cockpit canopy, and, with his helmet face-plate frosted suddenly by contact with the icy air, lunging into the void. His parachute opened automatically and he was picked up with an aching head but otherwise unhurt by a group of astonished Russian villagers. Among the items later recovered from the wreckage of his plane were cameras, film, radio-receiving and recording instruments — as well as the destructor which he had never managed to operate.

So much compromising material had survived the crash that Powers had no alternative to pleading guilty to espionage. The charge carried a maximum sentence of death, and his best course was one of damage limitation. His aim (he later wrote) was to make himself out to be a kind of 'airplane jockey' more than a spy; someone 'paid to fly along an assigned route flipping on and off switches as indicated on a map, with little knowledge of the results of my actions, and even less curiosity'. In this he was largely successful;

Prosecutor: On your plane there was aerial reconnaissance photo equipment. What instructions were you given?

Powers: I was not given any special instructions to operate the equipment. I was to turn switches on and off as indicated on the chart.

Prosecutor: With what purpose did you switch on the equipment?

Powers: I was instructed how to do this. It was indicated on the map that the equipment was to be turned on.

Prosecutor: Defendant Powers, you probably know the purpose for which you had to turn off and on the equipment?

Powers: I could very well guess the purpose for which I turned on and off the equipment. However, to be very exact, I would have to say no.

The prosecutor, Roman Rudenko, who was the chief Russian prosecutor at Nuremberg, was no fool, however. He knew how to make capital out of this stance.

Prosecutor: With the same ease you could have pulled a switch to release an atom bomb?

Powers: It could have been done. But this is not the type of plane for carrying and dropping such bombs.

The court gasped with indignation at the pilot's apparent complacency. And there were mutters, too, when his survival kit was examined. For example, he had been carrying a .22 ten-shot silent pistol. Powers claimed it was a hunting weapon for use if forced to live off the land; Rudenko replied that it was obviously an assassination weapon for use against Soviet citizens. Then there was the famous suicide pin, concealed in the silver dollar. It had contained curare, and the prosecution dwelled lovingly on its lethal potential. An expert testified:

'An experimental dog was given a hypodermic prick with the needle extracted from the pin, in the upper third part of the left hind leg. Within one minute after the prick the dog fell on his side, and a sharp slackening of the respiratory movements of the chest was observed, a cyanosis of the tongue and visible mucous membranes was noted. Within ninety seconds after the prick, breathing ceased entirely. Three minutes after the prick, the heart stopped functioning and death set in.'

In the final speech for the prosecution, Rudenko described Powers as no ordinary spy but a 'specially and carefully trained criminal'. The prosecutor portrayed a callous operative, equipped with poison needle and assassin's gun, who would drop an atom bomb on the Soviet Union without a qualm. And he asked that a strict, warning sentence be passed; not death but 15 years' imprisonment.

Powers's defence, represented by Mikhail Grinev, could scarcely be described as vigorous. During the trial he had neither challenged the facts nor the charges raised by the prosecution. Grinev's task in the propaganda exercise was to attack the United States by a different angle. Powers, he said, was only a pawn in Washington's villainous game. The real criminals who should be in the dock were the leaders of the American military establishment, and Allen Dulles, head of the CIA. Grinev stressed as extenuating circumstances the 'mass unemployment' and corrupt materialist values prevailing in the United States. Let the verdict be lenient, he pleaded, as yet another example of the humaneness of Soviet justice.

In the event, Gary Powers was sentenced to ten years' imprisonment, and served only two of them before being exchanged for the Soviet master spy, Rudolf Abel.

The U–2 incident had rocked the world, and proved a revelation in many ways. To begin with, a US president had been caught lying: the public had assumed that peacetime spying was a Russian vice; clearly the West was deeply engaged in it too. The experts had believed that Russia lacked the missile technology to shoot down a plane at 68,000 feet; that myth was also scotched now. And given the damaged reputation of the United States, there were many who declared that Powers had somehow failed in his duty: he should have used the suicide needle rather than plead guilty to espionage in a Soviet court.

This was grossly unfair. The President had already told the world that the U–2 was on an espionage flight. How could Powers plead not guilty? He had been hired as a pilot, not a secret agent, and his CIA contract specifically stated that in the event of capture he was free to tell the truth about his mission. As for the famous silver coin with its deadly hypodermic, Powers was not even obliged to take it on his flight, let alone use it in event of capture. A Senate Armed Services Committee investigated the whole affair after Powers's return to the United States, and CIA director John McCone stated categorically:

'In regard to the poison needle which was prominently displayed at the trial at Moscow, it should be emphasized that this was intended for use primarily if the pilot were subjected to torture or other circumstances which in his discretion warranted his taking his own life. There were no instructions that he should commit suicide and no expectation that he would do so except in those situations just described, and I emphasize that even taking the needle with him on the plane was not mandatory, it was his option.'

The committee fully exonerated Powers, but the trial had helped to frame new modes of thought in the coming decade. The Cold War no longer looked quite so much a struggle between good and evil; a grey moral zone was emerging. In the 1960s, people in the West discovered a 'credibility gap' between what their own leaders said and did. For better or worse, a new realism — even cynicism — became prevalent in international affairs. It was reflected in a remark of Eisenhower's press secretary, James Hagerty, when asked on television what were the lessons of the U–2 crisis.

'Don't get caught,' he said.

A Judicial Error

'While demonstrating how a revolver could have been used by the defendant on trial in a shooting case, Judge D. F. Sotomayor, of the Tijuana Court of the First Instance, shot himself behind the left ear and died an hour later. Under the impression that court attachés had removed the cartridges from the revolver, Judge Sotomayor placed the muzzle of the revolver under his left ear and pulled the trigger.'

PRESS DISPATCH, TIJUANA, 1926

Fall of a hero

SIR WALTER RALEIGH

Soldier, courtier, pirate, poet, explorer . . . Sir Walter Raleigh was the most astonishing of the Elizabethan sea dogs. Born in 1554, he played his part in the defeat of the Armada, led a search for El Dorado and founded the first colony of Virginia. It was Raleigh who reputedly brought back the potato and tobacco plants; Raleigh who commanded at the sack of Cadiz, at which the Spanish treasure fleet was destroyed. Sir Walter was seriously wounded in the fray, and you might think that his achievements would have guaranteed the Crown's gratitude for life. But not so. The Tudor Court was a dangerous playground for adventurous spirits, and even under Elizabeth Sir Walter's fortunes had never been secure. In 1603, when James I came to the throne, things turned very much worse; Sir Walter Raleigh was accused of high treason.

The charge was almost certainly trumped up, and instigated by a vindictive Court enemy, Robert Cecil. But the affair revolved around two conspiracies, which were real enough, and hatched at the time of James's accession. The first, known as the Bye Plot, was a hair-brained Catholic scheme in which Raleigh played no part at all. The second, or Main Plot, was more shadowy and conceived by Lord Cobham, a friend of Raleigh, who was Warden of the Cinque Ports.

Cobham was a headstrong and unstable character who detested the new king and made no secret of it. He had opened clandestine negotiations with the Spanish ambassador for the Netherlands, hoping to achieve peace between England and Spain. It is said, too, that he planned to put Arabella Stuart, James's cousin, on the throne.

How much did Raleigh know of all this? Questioned by the Council, he admitted that Cobham had offered him 10,000 crowns to help promote a peace with Spain. But Raleigh claimed that he paid no attention to the offer, dismissing it as one of Cobham's boastful idiocies. As far as the secret talks with the ambassador were concerned, Raleigh could say only that he suspected they might have taken place — he knew nothing more certain than that. The truth is that Raleigh may have been taken further into Cobham's confidence than he admitted; but he would not have been party to the scheme underfoot, for he was a notorious enemy of Spain.

In all events, Robert Cecil, investigating the affair, went to Cobham and confronted him with what Raleigh had said. Cobham, clearly feeling that Raleigh had betrayed him, replied in a rage that Sir Walter was behind the whole scheme. The charge was patently false, but it was enough to send Raleigh to the Tower.

Raleigh was in serious trouble. It was vital that Cobham withdraw his accusation, but as both men were now imprisoned in the Tower direct communication was impossible. Nevertheless, the resourceful Sir Walter came up with a solution. He wrote a letter to Cobham imploring that he tell the truth and, wrapping it with string tied around an apple, got a servant to toss it through Cobham's window in the Wardrobe Tower.

Cobham later slid his reply under his cell door, and when it reached Sir Walter the sea dog was delighted. Cobham had retracted his accusation — and expressed bitter regret at having made it. Armed with this letter, Sir Walter must have awaited the coming trial with less trepidation than before.

The trial opened on 17 November 1603, and was held at Winchester Assizes. Raleigh was driven there by coach through streets lined with angry mobs. Reviled as a traitor, the former hero was pelted with filth and, in mockery, with tobacco pipes. On arrival he found himself facing four judges and a jury of hostile commissioners who included Robert Cecil himself. Also ranged against him was a formidable adversary in Sir Edward Coke, the Attorney General.

The trial began as Coke launched into a lengthy account of the Bye Plot, and since no shred of evidence connected Raleigh with that conspiracy, the clear aim was to smear the prisoner by association. Raleigh would have none of it. 'Mr Attorney,' he interrupted, 'I pray you to whom, or to what end, speak you all this? I protest I do not understand what a word of this means, except it be to tell me news.' When Coke replied with bluster, Raleigh persisted in asking for hard facts: 'Prove against me any one thing of the many that you have broke.'

'Nay,' retaliated Coke, 'I will prove all; thou art a monster; thou hast an English face, but a Spanish heart.' This to the hero half-lamed by wounds sustained at the sack of Cadiz! Raleigh kept his temper, meeting every insult with imperturbable calm. And when permitted to deliver his defence he gave a masterful speech. Far from wanting to see peace with Spain, he said, he had only recently presented a treatise to His Majesty arguing that peace should be avoided. There was only one witness against him: Cobham. And Raleigh's repeated demand was that the witness should be brought into court so that he could face his accuser directly. The request was refused, however, on the grounds that Cobham was party to the plot.

As the trial dragged on, it became clear that the Crown's flimsy case was sustained chiefly by hearsay and abuse. Raleigh was 'a spider of Hell', 'an odious fellow', 'the confidentest traitor that ever came to the bar'.

The prisoner's dignified manner impressed everyone present, and Coke's thrusts were met, increasingly, with hisses and groans. But under the law as it stood, Raleigh could by no means be sure of an acquittal. He pinned his hopes on the letter in his pocket — Cobham's retraction written in the Tower. And, as the trial neared its end and he prepared to play his trump card, he met with a horrible surprise. The prosecution had a higher card still. The shiftless Cobham had changed his tune again and, in a letter to the Lords, had retracted his retraction! He now claimed that Raleigh had asked for a £1,500 annual pension from Spain to work as a Spanish agent!

This startling new charge sank Raleigh's defence. Deny it as he might, enough of the mud now stuck fast to seal his conviction. The jury was out for only a quarter of an hour; and returned to find the prisoner guilty of high treason. Sir Walter listened with the same dignified calm he had exhibited throughout the trial as the Lord Chief Justice delivered the appalling sentence:

'That you shall be had from hence to the place whence you came, there to remain until the day of execution; and from thence you shall be drawn upon a hurdle through the open streets to the place of execution, there to be hanged and cut down alive, and your body shall be opened, your heart and bowels plucked out, and your privy members cut off, and thrown into the fire before your eyes; then your head to be stricken off your body, and your body shall be divided into four quarters, to be disposed of at the king's pleasure: And God have mercy upon your soul.'

It is said that, on his deathbed, one of the judges confessed, 'never before had English Justice been so disgraced as in the case of the trial of Sir Walter Raleigh'. As news of the proceedings circulated, public hatred of Raleigh turned to adulation. And perhaps it was Sir Walter's new popularity that caused James I to stay the hero's execution.

The King stage-managed a macabre melodrama. On 10 December at Wolversey Castle, Winchester, Cobham and two Bye Plot conspirators were led to the scaffold through a dark winter's drizzle. Raleigh was ordered to watch from his cell, since his own hour was soon to come. But when the three prisoners had said their prayers and readied themselves for the ordeal, the sheriff surprised them by announcing a last-minute reprieve. The conspirators almost fainted with gratitude and Raleigh, watching from his window, was left entirely baffled as to his own fate. Dared he raise his hopes too? As the courtier Sir Dudley Carleton later declared, he must have had 'hammers working in his heart to beat out the meaning of this stratagem'. It was some time before Raleigh learned that he too had been granted a reprieve.

Raleigh spent almost 13 years in the Bloody Tower (there writing his *History of the World*). He never gave up hope of winning his freedom, and eventually did find a way to reach the king's heart. He appealed to James's avarice, promising that if given his liberty he would, at his own cost, fit out an expedition to the region of the

Orinoco River, where Raleigh believed a fabulous gold mine to be located. The King, he asserted, could have all the riches found.

In March 1616, after much deliberation, James agreed to the enterprise. Without pardoning Raleigh, he did permit him to leave the Tower. Sir Walter was now 64 and a sick man, yet, helped by his friends, he raised the money to equip a small fleet and set sail for Guiana. It proved a calamitous expedition: the mine was never found, fighting broke out with the Spaniards and Raleigh's son died in the conflict. Eventually, after fevers and mutinies, the grizzled sea dog returned to Plymouth with only one ship — to face the wrath of King James.

He had to die. Spanish influence, now strong at Court, saw to that. But for what crime could he be executed? In the end, James revived the death sentence for treason which had been passed on him long ago at his trial. And so, on 29 October 1618, having been condemned, reprieved, imprisoned for 13 years, released to search for gold and condemned again when he failed to find it, Sir Walter Raleigh at last walked to the scaffold.

The prisoner was, at least, given the dignity of a beheading. Raleigh greeted the executioner in friendly fashion and asked to see the axe. Running his finger along the edge, he observed, 'This is a sharp medicine; but it is a sure cure for all diseases.' His courage never faltered. Before laying his head on the block he instructed the executioner, 'When I stretch forth my hands, despatch me.' Refusing a blindfold, he then prayed in quietness for a moment. And then he stretched out his hands.

Astonished by such bravery on the scaffold, the executioner could not bring himself to strike. Again Sir Walter stretched out his hands: 'What dost thou fear?' he asked. 'Strike, man, strike!'

The axe fell, twice, on the last of the great Elizabethans. Everyone present was amazed at the quantity of blood that issued from his aged neck.

Sir Walter Raleigh

Gunpowder, treason and plot GUY FAWKES

At midnight on 4 November 1605, a party of soldiers under the command of Sir Thomas Knevett entered the cellars beneath the House of Lords at Westminster and there seized Guy Fawkes, conspirator. With him were taken 36 barrels of gunpowder, which had been hidden under a mass of coals and wooden faggots, with a heap of rocks and iron bars included to increase the destructive effects of the blast. No one could deny that, as conspiracies go, the Gunpowder Plot was an ambitious conception. The goal was to blow up the Parliament on the day of the King's Speech: King James, his Lords and Commoners — all were to perish in the explosion.

'This may well be called a roaring, nay, a thundering sin of fire and brimstone,' fumed the King when he finally addressed Parliament and gave thanks for divine deliverance. And of course, Guy Fawkes, whose name has won a dark immortality through the plot, did not dream up the whole scheme alone.

In fact, the conspiracy was the brainchild of Robert Catesby and an assortment of other well-born Catholic gentlemen. Guy Fawkes, aged 35, was of somewhat humbler birth, a Yorkshireman who had served for some time in the Spanish army. It was because of his courage and his military training that he was brought into the plot, which evolved over several months. But if his nerve was cool, he was as fervent as the others in his Catholic faith and his desire to see it re-established in England.

There was an element of pure comedy about the original plan. The plotters decided to tunnel their way from a rented house in Westminster to the underground wall of the nearby House of Lords; then they would dig their way through its 11 feet of solid masonry. They toiled furtively at the project for many weeks before discovering that it was unnecessary. The vast cellar spaces beneath the Palace of Westminster were in fact rented out for storage space to the general public! All that the conspirators had to do was select a vault directly under the House of Lords, and take out a lease on it!

After they had rented the cellar as a warehouse, the rest proved fatally easy. The plotters just moved in their barrels of gunpowder by night, and covered them up with firewood. It was agreed that Fawkes, the military man, would light the gunpowder with a slow fuse which would give him 15 minutes to flee the scene. He would then board a waiting ship and escape by sea to Flanders. Meanwhile, his fellow conspirators would kidnap the royal children and spark a national rebellion while the authorities were still reeling from the explosion.

Unfortunately for the plotters, someone betrayed their cause. A now famous anonymous letter was written to the Catholic Lord Mounteagle, warning him to stay away from Parliament on the day of the Opening. The letter mentioned no names, and referred only enigmatically to the coming 'event'. But its implications were sinister: 'they shall receive a terrible blow, the Parliament, and yet they shall not see who hurts them'. Mounteagle took the letter to the King's ministers, and James himself is said to have cracked the mystery of its meaning — a bomb plot was afoot.

On the morning of 4 November, the Lord Chamberlain toured the cellars on the pretext of a routine inspection. He found Fawkes there in a corner, with his large pile of faggots, and asked casually what all the fuel was for. The conspirator replied noncommittally that it all belonged to his master Mr Thomas Percy. Now, Percy was a well-known Catholic courtier and in fact a fellow conspirator. Fawkes realized that the authorities must have guessed that something was up, and he dashed off to warn his companions. Some fled into the country; but Fawkes was ordered back to the cellar, and like a good soldier he obeyed. When the men came later to arrest him, he cannot have been taken entirely by surprise.

On arrest, Guy Fawkes was carried off to Whitehall, where in the royal bedchamber he was interrogated by King James and his council. From there he was conveyed to the Tower, and to an ordeal whose intensity can be guessed at through the ghastly transformation of his handwriting.

When first questioned, Fawkes had refused to admit to his guilt or to name any accomplices. He signed a document to that effect with a confident 'Guido Fawkes'. But the King noted that 'our well beloved Guido Fawkes' was proving obstinate, and should be more closely questioned. And the nature of close questioning in those days was not pleasant.

There was a second interrogation session. This time, Fawkes did give an outline of the plot, while refusing to name any names. His confession is signed with a frail and shaking hand that hints at horrors endured.

After a third session of interrogation, Fawkes broke and told everything. The signature on this document is little more than a trembling scrawl that begins with a G and falters away into nothingness. The prisoner made no attempt to write his second name – he appears to have been tortured to the threshold of death. Nevertheless, Guy Fawkes had held out until 9 November, by which time his accomplices had all in fact been seized already, or killed resisting arrest.

Guy Fawkes and six others were tried before a special commission in Westminster Hall on 27 January 1606. It was an elaborate occasion, designed to celebrate the King and to execrate his enemies more than to debate questions of innocence or guilt. The opening speech for the prosecution referred to a treason 'of such horror and monstrous nature that before now the Tongue of Man never delivered, the Ear of Man never heard, the Heart of Man never conceived, nor the Malice of Hellish or Earthly Devil ever practised . . .' and continued in the same bombastic vein. In fact, Guy Fawkes himself is barely mentioned in the trial records, except for a passage in which the judge seems puzzled as to why he had changed his plea from not guilty to guilty. The prisoner, it is reported, gave a barely comprehensible reply.

When sentence of death was passed on the conspirators it took the conventional form for treason. The prisoners were to be hanged, drawn and quartered. The House of Commons was not happy about this; it had asked permission to try the prisoners so that it could mete out a more severe punishment. But considering the appalling cruelty of the orthodox method, it is hard to imagine what more severe penalty could be devised.

On 31 January 1606, Guy Fawkes was led to his death in the company of three of his fellow plotters: Thomas Winter, Ambrose Rokewood and Robert Keyes. They were dragged on hurdles through the streets, from the Tower to Westminster, where a scaffold had been erected. Then the prisoners were hanged, cut down alive and disembowelled, their entrails being drawn out and burned before them. Finally, each prisoner was hacked into four pieces.

Because of his leading role in the affair, Guy Fawkes was made to go last, so that he might witness the suffering of his fellows. He made a brief speech of repentance and, being weak from illness and his earlier torture, needed help to mount the ladder.

The king who had to die CHARLES I

When Charles I was sentenced to death, the public executioner refused to carry out the beheading. Nobody, it seemed, wanted to go down in history as the man who severed the royal neck. And so, on the morning of 30 January 1649, at the black-draped scaffold in Whitehall, Charles met a headsman who not only wore a mask but a wig and false beard too. It was a curious touch, contributing an element of macabre charade to the solemnities. But then, the trial itself had been a stage-managed affair: its purpose was not really to try the King but to pass the death sentence upon him.

Charles had to die. Long before the court was even constituted, Cromwell and his supporters had decided he must perish. For what else could be done with him? Captured by Parliamentary forces and held at Carisbrooke Castle on the Isle of Wight, King Charles was an embarrassment to the new rulers of England. While the King lived he was a figurehead in whose cause renewed fighting would inevitably break out sooner or later. No, the King had to die and the only question was how: by assassination? A discreet poisoning, perhaps? In the end, most of Cromwell's supporters came to favour the idea of a public trial which, in a contemporary's words, would 'teach all kings to know that they were punishable for the wickedness of their lives'.

And so, on Tuesday, 30 January 1649, the King was conducted by barge to Westminster Palace and led to the Great Hall, where the specially convened Court was waiting. Everyone understood the historic significance of the occasion; such a trial had no precedent, and to share the burden of responsibility, 135 Special Commissioners had been appointed. Of these, however, barely half stood up to be counted in the Hall that day. Some were absent through cowardice; some disapproved of what was afoot, and in this category were men like Lord Fairfax, commander in chief of the Parliamentary forces during the Civil War. A highly successful general, Fairfax had become convinced that the trial would be rigged and refused to take any part in it. When his name was called in the Great Hall, his wife bravely shouted from the gallery that Lord Fairfax 'was not there in person, that he would never sit among them, and that they did him wrong to name him as a commissioner'.

Nevertheless, the trial went ahead. Lord President of the Court was a lawyer named John Bradshaw, who wore a bullet-proof hat for the occasion. The judges' benches were draped with scarlet; the Sword and Mace lay crossed on a table carpeted by a rich Turkey rug; the Hall itself was so jammed with soldiers that despite the open doors at the back very few ordinary citizens were able to enter. Charles arrived in due course and made his way down the central aisle, dressed in black and carrying a silver-headed cane. According to the official report he looked sternly round the assembly, sat down on the crimson velvet chair reserved for him, and, by failing to remove his hat, showed that he had no respect for the Court.

After the preliminaries, the chief prosecutor, a Mr Cook, read a long document which charged Charles Stuart with treason and high demeanours which included making himself a tyrant and maliciously waging war against Parliament and the people. The King listened in silence except at the end when, charged with being 'a tyrant and a murderer', he suddenly laughed aloud. The President then asked for his answer to the charges, and King Charles replied, 'I would know by what power I am called hither. When I know by what lawful authority I am called I shall answer.'

Bradshaw replied that he was being tried in the name of the people of England, 'of which you are elected king'. Indignantly, Charles replied, 'England was never an elective kingdom, but an hereditary kingdom from near these thousand years, therefore let me know by what authority I am called hither.'

There followed several crisp exchanges. The King demanded to know what right the assembly had to try him; Bradshaw reprimanded him for challenging the Court's authority. And with the pattern of the trial set in these opening moves, the president called a halt for the day.

When the proceedings were resumed on the following Monday the King again refused to answer the charges, and the same dispute erupted again. On the third day, the prosecution moved for a quick judgement on the grounds that, by refusing to answer the charges, the King was effectively confessing his guilt. Bradshaw gave the King one more chance to make a formal answer, and when Charles remained obstinate, the prosecution was allowed to bring forward its witnesses.

In the days that followed some two dozen witnesses were called, mostly from the Parliamentary army, to establish that the King had started the war when he raised his standard at Nottingham in August 1642; and that he subsequently took part in the fighting in person. Some claimed to have seen the King on horseback, or with drawn sword in his hand. What today might be categorized as a 'war crime' was also reported by a witness named Humfrey Brown, who claimed that the King had condoned an attack on surrendered Cromwellians in Leicester, saying 'I do not care if they cut them three times more, for they are mine enemies.'

When the evidence had been heard, the court proceeded to the business of passing sentence. It took a whole day to draft the required document, which was read in Westminster Hall on 27 January. By now, Cromwell's soldiers were growing impatient, and as the King entered the Hall loud cries of 'Justice!' and 'Execution!' were heard.

Bradshaw embarked on a long oration, waving aside interruptions from the King as well as protests from the indomitable Lady Fairfax. He itemized a catalogue of treasons, including all the 'murders, rapines, burnings, spoils, desolations, damage and mischief to this nation', resulting from the Civil War. And he concluded that, 'for all which treasons and crimes this Court doth adjudge that the said Charles Stuart is a tyrant, traitor, murderer and a public enemy, and shall be put to death by the severing of his head from his body'.

After the sentence was read, no last word was permitted from the King. When Charles called out, 'Will you hear me, sir?' Bradshaw replied in the negative. When the King persisted, the president simply repeated the command, 'Guard, withdraw your prisoner!' The King was dragged, still protesting, from the Hall amid the spits and jeers of the soldiers.

Two days after the trial was over, Charles said a moving farewell to his younger children; whatever his faults, all have agreed that he was a kindly family man. On 29 January, the death warrant was signed (by Cromwell and 68 others), ordering the sentence to be carried out the next day in the open streets before Whitehall.

On the fateful morning, Charles was woken before dawn, and is said to have dressed with great care. He particularly asked for a warm shirt so that he should not be seen to shiver from the cold, 'which some observers will imagine proceeds from fear'. On the scaffold, he was dignified, delivering a short speech in which he held fast to his principles of kingship. He said that he 'did not believe that the happiness of people lay in sharing government'. 'Subject and sovereign', he said, were 'clean different'.

Then, on the advice of the executioner, Charles tucked his hair into his silk cap. He exchanged a few words with the headsman and knelt to put his head on the block. After a moment's prayer, he gave a sign that the blade should fall.

It says much for the nerve of the anonymous executioner that, in that moment of historic drama, he did not falter. His aim was true: with a single blow he cut the King's head clean from his body.

The crowd groaned, long and low. The King's head was held up for all to view. Then began a frenzied surge to the scaffold by spectators eager to dip handkerchiefs in the royal blood for souvenirs.

The exile on Devil's Island ALFRED DREYFUS

The case against Captain Alfred Dreyfus was rubbish from the start — rubbish in the most literal sense. As part of routine surveillance, charladies at the German Embassy in Paris were bribed to sort through the wastepaper baskets of the German staff and pass on any letters, however crumpled, to the French counter-espionage service. On 26 September 1894, the elderly Mme Bastiane became the most famous charlady in world history; her rubbish collection yielded a document which ripped France in two and brought the nation to the brink of civil war. She had found a note — thereafter known as the *bordereau* (memorandum) — which listed five items of military information that an anonymous writer was offering to sell to the Germans.

The *bordereau* was unsigned, and the secrets offered were not in themselves of high importance. But someone in the French officer corps was spying for France's bitterest enemy and, from the evidence of the note, had clearly been doing so before. In looking for a culprit, counter-espionage alighted first on Captain Alfred Dreyfus, and they never looked any further.

For Dreyfus was a Jew, the son of a wealthy family of Alsace textile manufacturers, and something of a phenomenon on the General Staff. The army considered itself an élite, aristocratic body — no Jew had penetrated its upper echelons before.

In fact, Jewishness was the only thing that his accusers had against Dreyfus; that and the fact that he was an artillery officer and the secret information offered for sale chiefly concerned big guns. Dreyfus was tricked into providing a sample of his handwriting, and, when it seemed to bear some faint resemblance to that on the *bordereau,* he was formally arrested.

The secret court martial, held in December, was a charade. M. Gobert, chief handwriting expert to the General Staff (and to the Bank of France), had been asked to compare Dreyfus's sample with that on the incriminating note. He flatly declared that the writing was not the same. This would not do at all as far as the investigators were concerned, so they looked elsewhere, calling on the celebrated Alphonse Bertillon of the Sûreté. He was a pioneer of police identification methods (but not a handwriting expert). Told beforehand that Dreyfus was unquestionably guilty, and being a firm anti-Semite, Bertillon gave the positive identification required.

Otherwise the case rested on the flimsiest possible evidence. One witness was permitted to testify that some nameless individual, an 'honourable person', had told him that Dreyfus was a traitor. Another described how, when accused of treason, 'the Jew went pale'. Dreyfus's fate was clinched when forged evidence was presented to the judges behind the back of Dreyfus's lawyer, by Major Henry, deputy chief of counter-espionage.

Found guilty, Dreyfus was sentenced to life imprisonment and subjected to ritual degradation. On 4 January 1895 the prisoner was brought out on to the parade ground of the Military Academy, where troops formed a hollow square around him. His officer's insignia was ripped from his uniform; his sword was broken and theatrically tossed to the ground. Then, in tattered jacket and cap, Dreyfus was marched around the square to face the jeers and hatred of the soldiery. From the outset he had declared himself not guilty, and now, enduring the march of shame, he shouted 'I am innocent!' with almost every step.

Captain Alfred Dreyfus

To serve his sentence, Dreyfus was sent to Devil's Island, in the notorious French penal colony of Cayenne, French Guiana. There, under heavy guard and in solitary confinement, he was left to rot away. Back in France, there were many who considered him lucky to have escaped execution.

There the matter might have rested, but for the protests of Dreyfus's family and the integrity of one man at the War Office: Lieutenant-Colonel Georges Picquart. Appointed head of counter-espionage in July 1895, Picquart found that leaks to the Germany Embassy were continuing. Another document was intercepted — an express letter which came to be known as the *petit bleu* — which clearly incriminated an officer named Esterházy. Investigating the suspect, Picquart obtained specimens of his handwriting — and was amazed by its similarity to the handwriting on the *bordereau*. The more he looked into it the more Picquart became convinced that Dreyfus must be innocent; Esterházy, a man of dubious past and often in debt, was the culprit in both cases.

Picquart informed his superiors. To his horror they seemed not to care: 'What has it got to do with you if a Jew is on Devil's Island?' queried General Gonse.

'But, surely if he is innocent . . .'

'If you say nothing about it, nobody will know any different.'

But Picquart refused to say nothing about it, and in fact proved such an embarrassment that in November 1896 he was removed from the staff and ordered off to Tunisia — and subsequently to an area of fierce fighting there where his death looked most likely to occur.

Picquart did not die in North Africa, and the Dreyfus family were also campaigning for a retrial. They too had concluded that Esterházy must be the real culprit; the case was becoming a public issue and provoked questions in Parliament. A bombshell was lobbed into the whole affair when *Le Figaro* published some letters written by Esterházy in which he openly expressed his hatred for the French army.

As a sop to public opinion, an inquiry and court martial were stage-managed for Esterházy; handwriting experts were even brought forward to testify that Dreyfus had disguised his own hand to make it *look* like Esterházy's! In January 1898, Esterházy was acquitted of treason and Picquart, ordered back to Paris, was gaoled on the charge of forging evidence against him.

It was at this moment that the famous novelist Emile Zola weighed in with the most famous newspaper manifesto of all time. Printed on the front page of *L'Aurore* and headed *J'Accuse!*, Zola savaged the whole list of people involved in the Dreyfus cover-up, from the government and the generals downwards. The result? Yet another trial — this time of Zola, who was found guilty of criminal libel. Fined and sentenced to a year's imprisonment, he twice appealed and, when all else seemed hopeless, fled across the Channel to continue his campaign from England.

The whole of France was now in a ferment over the Dreyfus affair, and the fate of the man on Devil's Island was almost forgotten as the battle lines were drawn up. Factions fought largely according to the traditions of left and right in French politics: for Dreyfus were the republicans, the anti-clericals, the Protestants, freemasons and Jews. Ranged in the anti-Dreyfus camp were the army, the monarchists, Catholics and anti-Semites. But there were more complex alignments, too, as families split and lifelong friendships were broken. To take just one example, the novelist Marcel Proust was both a Jew and a fervent campaigner for Dreyfus. But his father, a fashionable doctor, was firmly anti-Dreyfus, being a personal friend of government ministers. When Marcel started organizing a petition of intellectuals on Dreyfus's behalf, his father would not speak to him for a week.

The turning point came when the War Office blundered by initiating the prosecution of Picquart. This inevitably led to a close scrutiny of all the documentary evidence against Dreyfus — and by now the army chiefs had built up a fat dossier. The trouble was that all the evidence was counterfeit; the intelligence officer Henry had taken it upon himself to compile a whole set of forged documents to incriminate Dreyfus and they were blatantly false. In August 1898, a new War Minister discovered Henry's conspiracy and ordered his arrest. Under questioning, the forger broke down and confessed — the next day he cut his throat with a razor. Esterházy clearly realized his number was up, and prudently fled the country.

The tide had turned; but it ebbed at a painfully slow rate. In June 1899, after four years on Devil's Island, Dreyfus was brought back to France to face the retrial his supporters had campaigned for. The prisoner's hair had gone grey; he looked a broken man. There was rioting in France at the time of the proceedings and an attempt was made to assassinate the defence lawyer, Labori. The fate of the nation itself seemed to hang in the balance as the seven judges considered their verdict. In the end, they decided by a majority of 5 votes to 2 that Dreyfus was guilty 'with extenuating circumstances'. He was sentenced to ten years' imprisonment.

It was a preposterous verdict: if Dreyfus was guilty, what circumstances could possibly extenuate his treachery? In reality, the court's finding was clearly designed to soften the blow to the army's morale, and defuse an incendiary situation. Only ten days later, on 19 September 1899, Dreyfus was pardoned by President Loubet.

That 'pardon' too was controversial: it implied some measure of guilt, and Dreyfus only accepted it on condition that he was free to go on fighting to prove his complete innocence. And so, eventually, he did. In 1906 the Rennes verdict was finally quashed and Dreyfus was fully exonerated. Restored to the army with the rank of major, he fought with distinction in World War I, from which he emerged a lieutenant-colonel and commander of the Legion of Honour.

One casualty of the war was Major-General Max von Schwartzkoppen, spymaster at the German Embassy in Paris. It is now known that Esterházy had furnished him with 162 important documents, and that the traitor was on the German payroll at 12,000 marks a month. Schwartzkoppen had been forbidden to speak at the time of the great *Affaire*, for French chaos only profited German military interests. But the burden of silence had obviously told on the one-time military attaché. In 1917, as Schwartzkoppen lay dying in a Berlin hospital, his wife heard him crying incessantly, 'Frenchmen, listen to me! Dreyfus is innocent! He was never guilty! Everything was intrigue and falsification! Dreyfus, I tell you, is innocent!'

Who started the Reichstag fire?

MARINUS VAN DER LUBBE

On the night of 27 February 1933, less than a month after Hitler became Chancellor in Germany, the Reichstag in Berlin was destroyed by fire. The historic building — Germany's Houses of Parliament — went up in a colossal conflagration whose flames seared deep into the pages of 20th-century history. For the Nazis claimed at once that the fire was the work of communists, a signal for revolution, and in the mood of public panic they were able to force through emergency laws which suspended civil rights and placed dictatorial powers in their own hands. Henceforth, any opposition was to be regarded as treason, and draconian penalties were introduced for many offences. Effectively, the Reichstag fire legalized the Nazi terror — it had suited them rather well.

Too well, perhaps, for their own version of events to be believable? Who really started the fire?

A young Dutch communist named Marinus van der Lubbe was arrested near the blazing building on the fateful night. A half-witted, shambling youth, he was reported to have been seized with household firelighters on him. Marinus, it appeared, had something of a history as a firebug and was alleged to have gone round Berlin in a drunken state saying that he wanted to burn down the Reichstag. And in September he was brought to trial along with his alleged accomplices: three Bulgarian communists named Dimitrov, Popov and Tanev; and the chairman of the Reichstag communists, Ernst Torgler.

It was supposed to be a show trial. Van der Lubbe pleaded guilty, and the judges were compliant to all that the Nazi authorities requested of them. And yet, though the court was happy to bend the law whenever necessary, Dimitrov turned in a brilliant performance which won acquittal for all the defendants except Van der Lubbe. In proceedings that lasted three months, the Bulgarian completely demolished the case against himself and his colleagues, and he did so with courage and style. Once, for example, when a witness could not be found, he asked pointedly whether the concentration camps had been searched.

Evidence was heard too which made the case against Van der Lubbe profoundly suspect. Experts testified, for example, that it was physically impossible for one man to have brought all the incendiary material — including petrol and chemicals — which had started the conflagration. The fire had begun in 30 different parts of the building and was blazing away merrily only 2 minutes and 5 seconds after Van der Lubbe was alleged to have entered.

He cannot have done it alone. Yet if the young Dutchman was working with accomplices, how had they managed to vanish so quickly from the scene of the crime?

Sentenced to death, Van der Lubbe was executed in April 1934. But the trial's critics never ceased to probe the fire's unexplained mysteries. It is now widely believed that the conflagration was the work of a squad of Nazis directed by Karl Ernst, leader of the Berlin SA, who brought the incendiaries in through an underground tunnel.

As for Van der Lubbe, the first attempt to have his case reviewed ended in 1967 with a very strange verdict. He was cleared of the charges of high treason and endangering the Reichstag; instead, it was ruled that he had merited only eight years in prison for arson.

This by no means satisfied the dead man's brother, Jan van der Lubbe of Amsterdam, and in December 1982 he was represented in a second review by Dr Robert Kempner. On this occasion, a Berlin court ruled that the whole trial had been a miscarriage of justice. 'It is not clear whether the Nazis simply manufactured the charges against him,' said Kempner. 'But if he was involved in starting the fire he was probably manipulated into doing so.'

The court's ruling had not cleared up the mystery of the fire; it simply denied the trial's validity. But at least, 48 years after he was executed, Marinus van der Lubbe was entitled to the benefit of the doubt.

Red Empress JIANG QING

She loved orchids and kept pet monkeys; in her private jet were silken bedsheets. The daughter of a concubine, a Shanghai film starlet in her youth, Jiang Qing hardly presented the obvious picture of a left-wing revolutionary. And yet she was a key figure in the gigantic human upheaval of China's Cultural Revolution. And as wife to Chairman Mao she helped to shape the lives of well over 800 million people.

It has been said that Jiang Qing always resented men, despite her widely rumoured promiscuity. Born in Shandong province in 1912, both she and her mother were mistreated by her father, and she grew up an outcast in the houses of wealthy male clients. By the age of 19, she had already been through two marriages and was the subject of lewd gossip when she made a film career under the name of Lan Ping (Blue Apple). But Jiang Qing had a vein of deep seriousness. In 1938 she met Mao Tse-tung, leader of the Chinese communists, and became his fourth wife — despite furious opposition from within the Party. In fact the marriage provoked a serious internal crisis, and only went ahead on the agreement that the former starlet would play no part in politics whatsoever.

For many years, Madame Mao honoured that promise. But it was broken in the early 1960s when she began radically reforming cultural life in Shanghai, especially in adapting traditional Chinese opera to make it serve modern revolutionary themes. Under a left-wing party boss, Shanghai was becoming a hotbed of reinvigorated revolutionism — and it was here, in 1966, that the first salvoes of the Cultural Revolution were fired.

The Great Proletarian Cultural Revolution was a massive onslaught, launched by Mao against traditional attitudes and bureaucracy which had been creeping back into Chinese life since the People's Republic was formed in 1949. Young people especially were mobilized as Red Guards to rekindle revolutionary zeal; many universities were closed and thousands of professors and party officials were hounded from their jobs to face persecution and disgrace. Several of the most prominent figures in Chinese life were publicly humiliated, and people all over the world became familiar with propaganda images of young Chinese, massed in their thousands, chanting loyalty to Mao and spouting his 'thoughts', which were encapsulated in the Little Red Book, which they waved.

Ferment was most intense during the years 1966–8, but the Cultural Revolution did not end definitively until Mao's death in September 1976. In that sense, it lasted a full decade, and throughout the period Jiang Qing belonged to the central group directing change: she was at the epicentre of the earthquake.

On Mao's death a power struggle broke out between the radical and moderate factions in China. Jiang Qing with three close associates in the leadership — Yao Wenyuan, Zhang Chunqiao and Wang Hongwen — represented the extreme leftist tendency, and, nicknamed the Gang of Four, they tried to seize the reins of government. They failed. Arrested in October 1976, they were held for four years pending trial.

The Gang of Four had pursued its own ends with vindictive fury in its day. Now that the tables had turned, it was inevitable that there should be a grand reckoning. And few can have savoured the situation more than the new vice-premier, Deng Xiao-ping. Twice disgraced under the Cultural Revolution, he had at one time been forced to work in a kitchen. But Deng was rapidly becoming the effective head of government and leading a dramatic programme of liberalization. He did not mince words about Mao's widow; she was a woman 'so evil, not enough evil can be said about her'.

The trial opened in November 1980 at the Public Security Headquarters in Peking. The crowd outside was bitterly hostile to the accused, who were brought in by the back entrance. Inside the building, before an audience of some 800 handpicked 'members of the public' a welter of charges was read out against the Gang of Four inciting them and six other defendants with ultimate responsibility for the persecution of exactly 729,511 people under the Cultural Revolution — of whom 34,800 died. On the bench sat a panel of 30 judges, and the session was opened by Chief Justice Jiang Hua — himself a victim of the Red Guards.

Jiang Qing's three associates looked pale and dispirited as they entered the iron-railed dock. In fact, little was heard from them in the days which followed; two collaborated fully with the new authorities in hope of lenient treatment, while the third, Zhang Chunqiao, refused to co-operate in any way — he did not utter a single word during the entire trial. So, from the outset, Mao's widow held all the limelight. Pouchy cheeked and bespectacled, the 67-year-old woman no longer looked a ravishing beauty. But she walked with pride and confidence into the dock — she was the star without question.

Defiance was the keynote of her performance. It was even reported that in a preliminary hearing Jiang Qing complained of the heat. When nothing was done, she stripped naked before the judges — only putting her clothes back on when officials turned off the heating. (The story may be true in its essentials; but it is unlikely that she got any further in undressing than undoing a tunic button or two.)

It was a remarkable trial. The authorities clearly took some trouble to project the image of fair and just proceedings, televised extracts were shown throughout China, as well as broadcast worldwide by satellite. Yet no foreign journalists were allowed to attend the hearings, and there are startling gaps in the record of precisely what went on.

Nevertheless the world saw plenty of Jiang Qing. On 26 November two young women from her earlier entourage came forward as witnesses to describe how, in 1974, Jiang had told them to poison Mao's mind against certain veteran communists. Mao's widow could be seen leaning nonchalantly against the rim of the dock and refusing to answer questions about the conspiracies of the late Marshal Lin Biao. Looking nonchalant was just one of her tricks; at other moments in the trial she would pointedly remove her hearing aid, as if indifferent to what was being said.

A whole range of charges was brought against her. One of the most persistent was that she had persecuted China's many ethnic minorities by, for example, suppressing the national costumes of Tibetans, Koreans and Mongols in favour of the familiar Maoist boiler suit (for herself, Madame Mao was known to detest the boiler suit, preferring to wear long black dresses of her own design). She had also forced Muslims to breed pigs, against their religion, further damaging race relations.

It was also heard how she had persecuted past acquaintances who had known her before her marriage to Mao. Allusions were made to her supposedly lurid private life, and it was said that she had organized raids on people's homes to recover compromising letters and documents.

Some of the most damaging evidence related to the framing of President Liu Shao-qi, who had been condemned as a reactionary during the Cultural Revolution and died mysteriously in prison. Mao's widow seems to have been particularly jealous of Liu's elegant US-born wife, who spent 11 years in prison. In court, Jiang Qing claimed to remember nothing about ordering her arrest on the trumped-up charge that she was a secret agent of the United States, Japan and Taiwan. Then a document ordering the arrest was produced and shown to bear Jiang Qing's signature. 'Yes, it's my handwriting,' Mao's widow admitted almost contemptuously. 'I recognize it.'

She also admitted to signing arrest orders for 11 other people connected with Liu, one of whom was to die under torture. Even Liu's cook had been arrested on the grounds that the excellence of his cooking had corrupted his employer. The unhappy man's skill had been a recipe for disaster. He appeared in court to testify that he'd been imprisoned for more than six years on the promise of an early release if he helped seal the fates of Liu and his wife.

It seems that Jiang Qing considered these and similar actions 'justifiable' in the battle against revisionism. But her replies were carefully edited, so that the whole truth is not known. For example, the main thrust of her defence seems to have been that she did everything with Mao's full consent, and was 'only obeying orders'. This was not a line that the new leadership wanted explored at length. In 1980, the cult of Mao was still very much alive, and although unprecedented official criticisms of him did emerge at the time of the trial, they came only in muted tones. Nor was there any official mention of the brief collaboration between the Gang of Four and Mao's nominal successor, Chairman Hua Guo-feng. Yet it was reliably reported that Jiang Qing did incriminate him for his actions in 1976; certainly, his fall from power rapidly accelerated during the trial and he was forced to resign. (This suited vice-chairman Deng very nicely: it has even been suggested that the whole trial was stage-managed to incriminate Hua.)

But the authorities did not censor Jiang Qing's extraordinary outbursts, which made the proceedings utterly compelling as a human drama. For example, on 12 December, Liao Mosha, an eminent essayist, described in the witness box how he had been condemned to

An angry Jiang Qing shouts at members of the court

eight years in gaol at the behest of Mao's wife. While giving testimony about the ordeal he appeared to break down, wiping his eyes. This clearly infuriated Jiang Qing. In sneering tones she hurled abuse at the man, shouting out that he was an 'enemy agent'. Twice the bench tried to call her to silence by ringing an electric bell; Jiang replied by rounding on the judges calling them 'renegades'. Eventually, she was grabbed by two burly young policewomen who hustled her from the court; the trial was suspended.

It was not the last time that the choleric widow had to be forcibly restrained. Similarly angry outbursts recurred later, when she was accused of persecuting another writer. Jiang denied the charge until a tape-recording from 1970 was played, in which she could be heard demanding evidence against her victim — even though she was told that none existed. Jiang Qing then acknowledged that the voice was her own, and tried to justify her position. The court, however, did not want to hear any justifications — she was shouted down by a woman prosecutor and again dragged from the court.

On 29 December, as proceedings drew to an end, the chief prosecutor called for the death sentence, which was carried out in China by a single bullet in the back of the head. In her own final statement, Jiang Qing lambasted her accusers, calling the new regime one of 'reactionaries', 'counter-revolutionaries', and 'fascists'. With ill-concealed emotion she proclaimed that, 'Arresting me and bringing me to trial is a defamation of Chairman Mao Tse-tung,' while, 'Trying me is tantamount to vilifying the people in their hundreds of millions.' How, she wanted to know, could the court take it upon itself to sentence Mao's spouse of nearly 40 years? She shouted Maoist slogans: 'It is right to rebel!'; 'Making revolution is no crime!' And once again she was dragged from the court, this time yelling defiantly that, 'You just want my head. I am prepared to die!'

It was a theme she took up at her next appearance when she challenged the court to have her publicly executed in Tian An Men Square, where Mao's mausoleum had been built. This was a bold and imaginative stroke which put her accusers firmly on the spot. What, after all, should be done with her?

Many in the new leadership probably believed that, for propaganda purposes, an execution should be avoided. But Mao's widow was making it very hard for them by her contemptuous defiance. Of course, she and her co-defendants were found guilty. But there was a considerable delay before sentence was passed — a delay marked by leftist bombings in Shanghai — the Gang of Four's power base.

Finally, on 25 January 1981, the court came up with a compromise not uncommon in China. Jiang Qing was given a suspended death sentence. Under Chinese law it provided for the prisoner to be gaoled for two years and then executed — if there was no sign of any repentance. The same sentence was passed on the still silent Zhang Chunqiao, while Wang received life and Yao was given a sentence of 20 years.

Mao's widow seemed unusually tense and subdued before sentence was passed. But immediately afterwards she began loudly protesting, and, forcibly handcuffed, she was removed from the courtroom for the last time, shouting Maoist slogans.

The whole trial had been remarkable — stage-managed, certainly, but nevertheless opening up windows into the soul of revolutionary China with its cliques, tensions and rivalries. It was Jiang Qing who, single-handed, turned what might have been a farce into a compulsive drama. Vituperative, defiant — and cruelly indifferent to the fate of her own victims — Mao's widow, the 'Red Empress', was also electrifying for her courage and conviction.

Two years after sentence was passed, the death penalty was lifted and life imprisonment substituted. But it was hard to believe that she had really repented. The newspapers reported only that she was being held in a high-security prison and understood to be kept in solitary confinement. It was said, too, that she passed the time in making little dolls, which earned her pocket money for small prison purchases.

CHAPTER 3
Curious Cases

Animals on Trial	The Portland Vase
Curious Libels	Carol Compton
Corinne Parpalaix	Gary Dotson

Bestial crimes

ANIMALS ON TRIAL

At Lavegny in France in 1457, a sow and her six piglets were taken to court and charged with having murdered and partly eaten a child. The sow was found guilty and condemned to death, but the piglets were acquitted because of their age, the bad example set by their mother, and the absence of direct proof connecting them with the crime.

A remarkable case; but by no means unique in the annals of the law. Animals were commonly hauled before the courts of medieval Europe, and in France alone, 92 cases are recorded between 1120 and 1740 (when a trial ended with the execution of a cow).

The correct legal forms were always observed. Domestic pets and livestock were usually tried in the common criminal courts, while wild animals fell within the Church's jurisdiction. Ecclesiastical trials might result in the penalty of death by exorcism and excommunication — often a lengthy business. If local people were annoyed by beastly miscreants, the creatures would be called three times to appear before the court. When they failed to do so, judgement was given against them by default. A warning would then be issued, ordering the animals to leave the district within a given time. If they failed to do so, the exorcism was solemnly pronounced.

The processes of the law are slow at the best of times. And since the churchmen were never quite sure that their exorcisms would work they were especially reluctant to pronounce them. One 15th-century lawsuit between the people of St Julien and a beetle colony lasted fully 42 years.

Part of the problem lay too in getting animals to obey summonses. Every effort was made to correctly identify the accused; at one famous case in Autun, the local rats were accused of wilful damage and written of as 'dirty animals in the form of rats, of a greyish colour, living in holes'. The trial of 1521 is celebrated in French legal history because it was in it that the great lawyer Bartholomew Chassanée made his name. He was appointed as defence counsel for the rats and threw himself into the fight with both skill and passion.

Why had his clients not appeared before the court on the appointed day? Chassanée first excused them on the grounds that the summons was incorrectly phrased, and should have specified all the rats of the diocese. Then he successfully pleaded for an extension of the deadline on the grounds that many of his clients were elderly and infirm rats for whom special arrangements had to be made. When the defendants failed to turn up for the third appointment, he explained that the rats were in fact most anxious to appear before the court but were being frightened off by the large number of malevolent cats kept by the plaintiffs. The court had a duty to protect defendants. Let all the cats be locked up with assurances that they would not molest his clients and the rats would most certainly appear.

The court accepted his plea. But the people of Autun would not agree to bind over their cats to keep the peace. The case was dismissed — Chassanée had won.

In Germany in 1499, the trial of a bear was delayed for many days on the grounds that it had a right to be tried by a jury of its peers (i.e. other bears). In Italy in 1519 some moles were charged with damage to crops, and sentenced in their absence to banishment. But the court was prepared to be considerate, promising safe conduct with an extension of 14 days to all expectant mothers and infant moles.

The courts were not always so understanding, however, and where charges of sorcery were involved an animal could expect no mercy. At Basle in 1474, a cock was tried before a court for having laid an egg. In vain did the defence plead that the act was harmless and involuntary, and as such not punishable by law. The prosecution contended that only through Satan could such an event be accomplished. The bird was a devil in disguise, and the hapless cock, with its egg, was burnt at the stake with all due form and solemnity.

Animals have not only appeared in the dock but in the witness box too. In Savoy, before its union with France, there was a law that stated that if you killed an intruder in your home at night, the act would be considered justifiable homicide. But the authorities worried that someone might deliberately entice another person to their home for the purpose of murdering them — afterwards claiming that the victim was a prowler. So a householder was not held to be innocent unless some animal such as a dog, a cat or a cockerel was produced from the house to bear witness. The owner of the house had to declare his or her innocence on oath before the creature. The law assumed that God would make the dumb animal speak rather than permit a murderer to escape justice.

A smashing case

THE PORTLAND VASE

The world's most valuable item of glassware, everyone agrees, is the famous Portland Vase, made in Italy at around the time of Christ, and on display at the British Museum. Barely 10 inches high, the piece is, quite literally, priceless; so completely unique that no sum can be quoted in valuation. And looking at this most delicate of the world's art treasures, it is hard to believe that, more than a hundred years ago, it was smashed to smithereens.

It happened at 3.45 pm on 7 February 1845. A number of visitors wandering around the Hamiltonian Room at the museum suddenly heard an ear-shattering crash. Everyone rushed to the ante-room where the vase normally stood in a display case mounted on an octagonal table. But the vase was not there — it was scattered in a hundred fragments on the floor.

Whodunit? The doors were immediately closed and a Mr Hawkins, the Superintendent, questioned the horrified visitors. Eventually he got round to one William Lloyd, theatrical scene painter from Dublin. 'Alone I did it!' the miscreant proudly roared. He had taken aim with a small item of sculpture picked up nearby, and when taken to Bow Street Police Station excused himself on the grounds of 'delirium, arising from habitual intemperance'. That is to say, he was drunk as usual.

The amazing feature of the incident, though, was that the law was almost powerless against the vandal. The existing Wilful Damage Act only provided for deliberate damage done to property worth up to £5; the penalties were a £5 fine or 2 months' imprisonment. Now, however hard it was to gauge the price of the Portland Vase, it was certainly worth more than £5. But the defect in the law was such that Lloyd could not be directed to pay anything for shattering the Portland Vase; instead, he was ordered to pay £5 for the glass case in which it had stood!

As it happened, Lloyd only had ninepence on him at the time, and so was hauled off to gaol. But he had served less than a week of his two-month sentence before an anonymous donor sent £5 to pay the fine. The vandal was freed, and having made his brief, ignominious bow in the spotlight of history, vanished backstage forever. The vase, however, was painstakingly restored in the months that followed, and it was not long before Parliament passed a special Act to protect works of art from similar outrages.

You can't say that!

CURIOUS LIBELS

When the young Liberace arrived in Europe in 1956 he came in inimitable style. At Cherbourg the pianist addressed a packed press conference from amid a forest of candelabra; from Southampton he and his entourage proceeded to London on a specially commissioned six-carriage train. At Waterloo Station, 3,000 women surged towards the entertainer's coach to scream and swoon and faint. For William Neil Connor, 'Cassandra' columnist of the *Daily Mirror*, it was all too much.

Liberace, he wrote, was a 'deadly, winking, sniggering, chromium-plated, scent-impregnated, luminous, quivering, giggling, fruit-flavoured, mincing, ice-covered heap of Mother Love'. Then the columnist really got into his stride:

This appalling man and I use the word appalling in no other than its true sense of 'terrifying' has hit this country in a way that is as violent as Churchill receiving the cheers on VE day. He reeks with emetic language that can only make grown men long for a quiet corner, an aspidistra, a handkerchief and the old heave-ho. Without doubt he is the biggest sentimental vomit of all time.

Fair comment? Connor had much more to say on the subject of Liberace, and when he followed up with a second article in similar vein, the entertainer brought out an action of libel against the columnist and Daily Mirror Newspapers Ltd.

In the course of the much-publicized seven-day trial, Liberace's lawyers declared that the diatribes were clearly intended to insinuate

Liberace seated at his piano

that Liberace was a homosexual ('fruit-flavoured' being among the terms commonly used at the time). Nevertheless, the proceedings were largely good-humoured and provided an occasion to explore the entertainer's flamboyant lifestyle: his income of more that $1 million a year; his 60 suits; his diamond-studded tailcoat; his piano-shaped swimming pool; his Mom; his fans; brother George on the maracas.

Bob Monkhouse and Cicely Courtneidge were among those who testified on Liberace's behalf, and the cause of 'Cassandra' was not assisted by the testimony of thriller writer Betty Ambler, who had interviewed him shortly before the court case. In the course of their conversation, Connor had allegedly said of the coming trial, 'It is going to be a lot of fun and Liberace will get a lot of money from the *Daily Mirror*, but it will be worth it for a week's publicity.'

In fact, Liberace was awarded £8,000 damages, and costs. The case had no serious implication except in illustrating how narrow is the line dividing what you can say in criticism from what you can't.

The classic in this context was a trial which opened in London in November 1878, and involved two of the most celebrated figures in the Victorian art world. One was John Ruskin, the writer and art critic; the other was James McNeill Whistler, an artist of genius whose modernist style did not meet Ruskin's approval. Following a visit to the Grosvenor Gallery, the critic virtually called Whistler an impostor, and likened his work to 'flinging a pot of paint in the public's face'.

Strong stuff; but libellous? The hot-tempered Whistler brought an action against the critic, and coming at a time of ferment in the arts, the trial seemed to embody the struggle between the adventurous new painting and the dry old art of the Academy. Whistler fairly leaped into the witness box and, under cross-examination, stated his case with haughty bravado. His *Nocturne* at the Grosvenor Gallery bore a price tag of 200 guineas!

Attorney General: Is that not what we, who are not artists, would call a 'stiffish' price?

Whistler: I think that may well be so.

Attorney General: Now, Mr Whistler, can you tell me how long it took you to knock off that *Nocturne*? I beg your pardon, I am using a term that applies rather to my own work. I should have said how long did you take to paint the picture?

Whistler (sarcastically): Oh no, permit me, I am too greatly flattered to think that you apply to work of mine a term that you are in the habit of using with reference to your own. Let us say then, 'how long did you take to knock off', I think that is it, 'to knock off that *Nocturne*?' As far as I remember, about a day or perhaps two days.

Attorney General: Oh, two days! The labour of two days, then, is that for which you ask 200 guineas?

Whistler: Oh, no, I ask it for the knowledge of a lifetime!

Wild cheers from the Whistlerites! And the painter continued to play to the gallery when asked by the Attorney General, 'Do you think now that you could make *me* see the beauty of that picture?' Whistler looked at the lawyer long and hard. 'No,' he concluded, 'do you know, I fear it would be as hopeless for the musician to pour his notes into the ear of a deaf man.'

In fact Whistler won the case, but was awarded only a farthing in damages — the trial ruined him financially. And libel actions have often gone horribly wrong for the plaintiff as the cases of Oscar Wilde (see page 108) and Gordon-Cumming (see page 102) illustrate.

In more recent years, football manager Tommy Docherty got himself into deep trouble by suing his former player Willie Morgan.

It happened in 1977, after Morgan had made some scathing remarks about Docherty on Granada TV's *Kick Off* programme. Docherty, he said, was 'about the worst manager there has ever been,' and, 'When he goes I think the rejoicing in Manchester will be like winning the cup again.'

Docherty tackled back with a libel action, and Morgan countered by specifying a whole set of allegations about the manager's behaviour. One of these concerned the way he had handled the transfer of Denis Law to Manchester City. On the fourth day of the trial, Docherty got entangled in a series of contradictory statements about the transfer and was asked under cross-examination, 'You told a pack of lies to the jury about this, didn't you?'

'Yes,' replied Docherty, 'it turned out that way.'

Oops. His case collapsed, he withdrew his action and was forced to pay Morgan's costs. Worse, Docherty was later taken to court on the criminal charge of perjury, and, though acquitted, cannot be said to have profited by looking to the law.

The costs of a libel action can be enormous. The largest sum ever awarded in Britain was more that £1 million, awarded to a Harley Street slimming specialist against the BBC and members of the *That's Life* team, including presenter Esther Rantzen. The programme, broadcast in June 1983, had in the doctor's words made him out to be 'an unscrupulous, profiteering quack'. The 87-day trial required the attendance of no fewer than 50 witnesses, mountains of complex medical testimony and armies of barristers and solicitors. Ironically, the case was also dogged by ill health: the prosecuting counsel began in a wheelchair because of an ailing leg; the BBC's solicitor appeared on crutches; the judge caught 'flu; a juror went sick, and the usher collapsed in court.

The case ended in April 1985 with a settlement out of court, the doctor receiving £75,000 damages. It fell only 14 days short of the record length set in March 1981 (by an unsuccessful libel case brought against the *Daily Mail* by the Moonies). And it was lucky that it ended when it did; everyone agreed that if it had continued it could have lasted till the end of the year.

The sheer size of an award does not count for everything. In 1937, novelist Graham Greene was sued by lawyers representing Shirley Temple for allegations which the writer had made in a review of her film *Wee Willie Winkie*. Greene had suggested that male audiences found the child star and her shortie kilt appealing for reasons that were not entirely innocent. An action followed — libel was admitted — and £3,500 were awarded in damages. The affair ruined *Night and Day*, the magazine in which the review appeared, and it ceased publication soon afterwards.

Film characters may themselves be libellous; that principle was firmly established in the 1934 case of Youssoupoff *vs* MGM. Metro-Goldwyn-Mayer had produced a film called *Rasputin the Mad Monk*, which featured a fictional couple called Prince and Princess Chegodieff. The real-life Princess Irena Youssoupoff won massive damages because, she alleged, the fictional princess was an obvious portrait of herself — and was shown having an affair with the hairy hypnotist. That was bad enough for MGM — but worse was to come when a real-life Prince and Princess Chegodieff subsequently turned up. The studio paid them too — out of court.

You can libel someone through almost anything — even a waxwork dummy. That was the finding in the case of Alfred Monson, leading actor in one of the great Victorian courtroom dramas.

Alfred John Monson, a tutor, was tried at Edinburgh in December 1893 for the murder of a youth named Cecil Hambrough. The circumstances were highly incriminating: Monson stood to profit financially by Cecil's death, and clearly lied to the court on several issues relating to his supposed 'suicide'. Nevertheless, the judge summed up with the now famous remark that, 'It is the business of the Crown to prove the case, and not for the defence to prove innocence.' A verdict of Murder Not Proven was given — a particularly Scottish institution indicating that though guilt was not proven, innocence had not been established either.

Monson was freed. But the case had fascinated the public, and a life-size effigy of the supposed murderer was set up in the ante-room of the Chamber of Horrors at Madame Tussaud's. In 1894, Monson sued the museum for libel and had the satisfaction of winning the case. The damages? Murder, they say, is an art — Monson got a farthing, like Whistler.

The strange case of the Scottish nanny

CAROL COMPTON

When 21-year-old Carol Compton entered the Livorno courtroom, the pressmen seemed to go mad. Journalists vaulted across tables and surged past police in attempts to reach the girl as she was led, wearing jeans and a crucifix, into the cage built for terrorists which served as her dock. The court had banned photographers, but still the cameras clicked and whirred, registering the pale, bewildered face of the accused. In the cage she chewed gum incessantly. Her mother snatched a kiss through the bars, calling, 'You're not scared, are you? I have been waiting for this for a long time. Get up and give them what for.

It was December 1983, and this was no ordinary case. For 16 months, young Carol Compton from Aberdeen had been held on charges of arson and attempted murder. But what fascinated press and public alike were the allegations, loudly aired in the Italian media, that she was a witch.

She had been held since August 1982, when she had been arrested on the island of Elba. Carol had worked there as a nanny for an Italian family, and it was alleged that shortly after her arrival two suspicious fires broke out — one of them threatening the life of a three-year-old child named Agnese. Before coming to Elba, Carol had worked for a household in the northern town of Ortosel. Three suspicious fires were said to have broken out there too. But it wasn't just the fires that captured the press's attention. It had been reported that all kinds of paranormal events occurred when Carol was around.

The case was heard by two professional and six lay judges, and from the outset the proceedings were chaotic. Apart from the antics of the pressmen, the courtroom acoustics were poor and Carol's thick Scottish accent presented problems for the interpreter. For example, she spoke on one occasion of a baby's 'cot'; it sounded like 'coat', and was translated as 'blanket'. She spoke of noises making her 'nervous'; the word was translated as *nervosa*, which means irritable. Complaints were made by a British Embassy official about the competence of the interpreter. At one point Carol abandoned translation and spoke directly to the bench in what little Italian she had picked up while in gaol.

Despite the problems, the trial went ahead and the issue of witchcraft soon came up. In early testimony, Carol's first employer had described how her maid in Rome spoke of a vase that had inexplicably fallen to the floor in Carol's presence; a picture of the Madonna had done so too. In court, the employer now admitted that the events could be explained in terms of normal accident. But the paranormal would not go away: a forensic expert from Pisa University claimed that the two fires he had investigated were 'phenomenal': they seemed to burn *downward* instead of up; 'they were created by an intense sort of heat, but not by flames'.

Later, the grandmother of little Agnese testified that strange things had happened at her home on Elba after Carol's arrival. A plate and a cake dish fell to the floor without apparently being touched. 'Good heavens, there are spirits in our home,' she claimed to have said at the time.

All very spooky — but not really very substantial. Throughout the trial the prosecutor himself tried to keep sorcery out of the case. Carol Compton, he said, was not being tried as a witch but on five counts of arson and one of attempted murder. There was nothing inexplicable

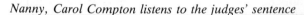

Nanny, Carol Compton listens to the judges' sentence

about the fires, he said: Carol Compton had started them. He could not be positive about the motive, but strongly suggested as a likely explanation that Carol might have lit the fires so that she could return to her boyfriend in Rome. In summing up he asked for a seven-year sentence, and criticized the media's impact on the proceedings. 'We have talked more fully about falling vases', he complained, 'than about the baby she is accused of trying to murder.'

The main defence counsel was similarly dismissive about the so-called paranormal element. And in the end no ducking stools or *autos da fé* were invoked. Carol Compton was found not guilty of attempted murder, and acquitted of one of the five arson charges. But she was found guilty on the four others (two of them being reduced to attempted arson). The Scottish nanny was sentenced to 2½ years' prison, meaning immediate release because of the long time she had already spent in pre-trial detention.

Carol Compton left Italy for home as soon as the trial was over. The judges subsequently issued a written explanation of their verdict, confirming that there was nothing paranormal about the case. In November 1984, an appeal on Carol's behalf failed, the Italian court upholding the original conviction.

Artificial insemination — a test case CORINNE PARPALAIX

Sperm banks, womb leasing, artificial insemination . . . the advances of modern medicine have created a wealth of new legal as well as moral problems. One of the most extraordinary cases to come before the courts was that of Mme Corinne Parpalaix, a Frenchwoman who desperately wanted a child by her husband. The problem was that her husband was dead.

Corinne had first met Alain in August 1981. He was a police officer who, shortly after they met, discovered that he had a serious illness. Told that he would require an operation which might leave him sterile, he decided first to make a deposit in a sperm bank known as Cecos — the Centre for the Study and Conservation of Sperm.

Alain's condition worsened afterwards. The couple married in hospital on 23 December 1983, but only two days later, on Christmas Day, he died.

Alain had left no written instruction about who was to inherit the sperm. But both his wife and his parents insisted that shortly before he died he had expressed a last wish to have a baby by Corinne. The sperm bank, however, refused to release his deposit without formal instructions from the Ministry of Health. And the Ministry declared that since the whole subject of artificial insemination was under review, no such instructions could be issued.

Corinne had recourse to the law, and in August 1984 a court at Creteil, just outside Paris, ruled that the sperm bank must hand the deposit over. Mme Parpalaix wept with relief when she heard the judgement. Thanking the court and her lawyers, she declared, 'This judgement makes me a happy woman.'

The case had made legal history. But sadly for Mme Parpalaix, her husband's illness had left him with sperm of very poor quality. Doctors decided that for the maximum chance of conception, they must insemi-nate her with the whole deposit at once — and in January 1985, it was announced that the attempt had failed.

As a sidelight on the legal complexities, it might be added that a baby would have been illegitimate. Under French law, a child must be born within 300 days of a husband's demise if paternity is to be acknowledged.

Rape and recantation GARY DOTSON

In 1979, 22-year-old Gary Dotson was tried and convicted for the rape, in the back of a car, of 16-year-old Cathy Crowell. Sentenced to more than 20 years, he was imprisoned at Dixon, Illinois.

Six years later, however, Dotson was released under sensational circumstances. His supposed victim announced that she had invented the attack. Now married with two children, Mrs Cathy Webb declared in an Illinois court that she had made up the rape story because she feared she might be pregnant after having sex with her boyfriend. Not wishing her foster parents to know of the affair, she had scratched herself and ripped her clothing before reporting the attack. Gary Dotson had simply been picked out from photographs the police had shown her. Now, she said, her religious faith had compelled her to speak out.

Reunited with his delighted mother and sisters, the released man expressed gratitude towards his former accuser, and declared that he bore her no bitterness. And there, in a mood of joy and reconciliation, the whole story seemed to have ended.

But it had a sting in its tail. Only a couple of weeks after his release, in April 1985, a judge in Markham, Illinois, refused to overturn Dotson's conviction and ordered him back to gaol. Judge Richard Samuels — the same judge who had presided at his 1979 trial — turned down Dotson's petition to quash his conviction, saying that he and the jury had been convinced of his guilt back in 1979, and he saw no reason to change his mind now. Recantation of evidence, said the judge, is always regarded as unreliable unless backed by strong corroboration. 'I don't know why Cathy Webb got up on the stand and told what she did. That's only known to her,' he said.

When he heard the verdict, Dotson pounded his fists on the table before him, while his family wept around. Cathy Webb, as she was led from the court sobbed: 'He is innocent, I lied in 1979.'

It was a very delicate problem. Recantations have to be treated with suspicion by the law, for witnesses might be bribed, or threatened, or have some ulterior motive in withdrawing evidence after a trial. In rape cases, the issue is even more sensitive. Many victims, traumatized by their experience and fearing that they will not be believed, are reluctant to testify anyway. How much more reluctant would they be if there was a risk of pressure being applied after a trial was over?

On the other hand, millions of TV viewers had seen the boyish prisoner and his former accuser, and believed their story to be true. Petitions were raised, floods of letters written, and outrage was expressed from all over the United States. Swiftly, an appeal for clemency was put before the state Governor, and early in May, Dotson was released on $100,000 bail.

The three-day clemency hearing in Chicago was televised live before the nation. It was not, technically, a retrial — Governor James Thompson was empowered only to grant pardon — but some 18 witnesses were brought forward, and both Dotson and Webb pressed for a full declaration of innocence.

In the end, Governor Thompson declared that he did not believe the recantation. Gary Dotson, he said, had been properly convicted, and the trial judge was quite right to refuse a new trial. Nevertheless, the Governor commuted the sentence to the six years Dotson had already served. 'Whatever the motive for Mrs Webb's recantation,' he explained, 'she is very clear that she does not want him to serve another day. I think I am entitled to take that into account.'

After all that had been said and heard, he concluded, the case was still troubling. 'It is very complex — in the end we don't know.'

A free man, Gary Dotson declared that he would go on fighting to clear his name. He appeared in public with Mrs Webb not long afterwards — they shook hands, in true American fashion, on a TV show.

CHAPTER 4

Matters of Public Concern

Lady Chatterley Trial   **Marie Stopes**
John T Scopes   **Caryl Chessman**
The Thalidomide Case   **Clive Ponting**

'Stark naked and dripping with raindrops . . .'

THE *LADY CHATTERLEY* TRIAL

There are 13 episodes of sexual intercourse in D. H. Lawrence's novel *Lady Chatterley's Lover*. We know, because the prosecutor at the book's famous trial carefully counted them for the benefit of the jury. Lawrence, he complained, went further than to describe mere bedroom scenes:

'One starts in my lady's boudoir, in her husband's house, one goes to the floor of a hut in the forest with a blanket laid down as a bed; we see them do it again in the undergrowth in the forest, amongst the shrubbery, and not only in the undergrowth of the forest, in the pouring rain, both of them stark naked and dripping with raindrops.'

Oh horrible, most horrible. *Stark naked and dripping with raindrops!* But worse was to come. The prosecuting counsel, Mr Mervyn Griffith-Jones, invited the jury to consider the sorry arithmetic: 'The word *fuck* or *fucking* occurs no less than thirty times. I have added them all up. *Cunt* fourteen times; *balls* thirteen times; *shit* and *arse* six times apiece; *cock* four times; *piss* three times, and so on.'

Those words were at the root of the problem. An expurgated version of Lawrence's novel had been available in Britain since 1928, but in

1960, when Penguin Books tried to publish the first full English edition, the Director of Public Prosecutions took action. Penguin was brought to trial under the Obscene Publications Act and 200,000 copies, priced at 3*s*. 6d, were held back from sale pending the court's decision.

Today, *Lady Chatterley's Lover* is generally agreed to be the worst novel Lawrence ever wrote; embarrassing not for its sexual explicitness but for weakness of plot and characterization. Lady Chatterley, the heroine, is feebly drawn while Mellors, her gamekeeper lover, is a grotesquely implausible creation. Nevertheless, for freethinking men and women at the threshold of the Swinging Sixties, the book's defence became a *cause célèbre*, and scores of prominent intellectuals offered to testify on its behalf.

The trial opened, amid intense public interest, on 20 October 1960. The Clerk of the Court referred to Penguin Books Ltd as the 'prisoner at the Bar', despite the fact that the great panelled dock at the Old Bailey's Court No. 1 was empty. Prosecution was brought under the Obscene Publications Act of 1959 which, only recently introduced, stated that a book might be considered obscene if its effect 'if taken as a whole is such as to tend to deprave and corrupt'. However, section 4 of the Act provided immunity for noted artworks: a person should not be convicted of an offence if the published material was 'for the public good on the ground that it is in the interests of science, litera- ture, art, or learning, or of other objects of general concern'.

The prosecution had its work cut out: even if the book were proved to be obscene, it could be excused on grounds of artistic merit.

Mr Mervyn Griffith-Jones, in opening, totted up his arithmetic of obscenity and went on to allege that the central characters were little more than 'bodies — bodies which continuously have sexual inter- course'. Was it, he asked, a book suitable for schoolchildren? 'Is it a book that is published at £5 a time as perhaps a historical document, being part of the works of a great writer, or is it, on the other hand, a book which is widely distributed at a price that the merest infant can afford?'

Perhaps a hint of snobbery, out of tune with the times, was betrayed by this line of argument. Clearly, the prosecution's worry had much to do with the fact that the book was going out as a cheap paperback, accessible to millions. And Mr Griffith-Jones showed his hand calami- tously when he posed his now celebrated question, 'Is it a book that you would have lying around the house? *Is it a book that you would even wish your wife or your servants to read?*'

It was an extraordinary blunder, suggesting that the jury — and indeed the whole reading public — consisted of wealthy gentlemen employing a sizeable domestic staff. Yet this was 1960, and three people on the jury were demonstrably women themselves. Perhaps the whole prosecution case was sunk irreparably by the gaffe: certainly,

1960, Londoners queuing to buy 'Lady C'

the jury members were visibly amused by the remark, which perfectly typecast Lady Chatterley's enemies as blimpish and fuddy-duddy.

The defence, in contrast, opened by establishing Lawrence's prominent place among the great writers of the 20th century. Far from tending to deprave or corrupt, said Mr Gerald Gardiner, the book was moral in purpose, enshrining the author's faith in physical tenderness between people as an alternative to the public worship of money and what Lawrence called the 'bitch-goddess, Success'. Explicitness about the body and its functions was essential to the author's purpose — the book was in no way obscene.

Before the trial could go further, the jury had to read the book itself. Where was this to be done? In the comfort of home, or in the jury room at the Old Bailey? The defence pressed for the former, urging, 'the jury rooms are jolly uncomfortable places. There are hard wooden seats, and anything more unnatural than twelve men and women sitting round a table on hard wooden chairs with a book is hard to imagine.'

The judge arrived at a compromise, ruling that the jury must read the book at the Old Bailey, but ordering that a special room be fitted out with deep leather armchairs. It took the slowest reader among the jury three days to finish the task — after that, witnesses could be called.

In all, 35 public figures came forward to speak for the defence: critics, theologians, teachers, writers and editors among them. It was the first time that defendants were permitted to bring witnesses on the literary and moral qualities of a book in an obscenity case, and many household names appeared before the court: Dame Rebecca West, E. M. Forster, Dilys Powell, Cecil Day Lewis, the Bishop of Woolwich and others. Less well known — but just as important to the defence — were figures such as Miss Sarah Beryl Jones, Classics Mistress at Keighley Girls Grammar School, who testified that *Lady Chatterley* was fit to be read by her charges.

Norman St John-Stevas, then a practising barrister and author of *Obscenity and the Law*, acknowledged, 'I would not say it was the best book Lawrence ever wrote,' but continued, 'I think it is a very well-written book and is a contribution of considerable value to English literature.' A Catholic, he added, 'This is undoubtedly a moral book.'

Another prominent politician of the future, Mr Roy Jenkins, MP, had been chief sponsor of the Obscene Publications Bill during its difficult progress through Parliament. He made it clear, before being cut off by the judge, that the prosecution was against the intention of the Act. He was asked if he considered the book literature:

Jenkins: Yes, it most certainly is. Indeed, if I may add, it did not occur to me in the five years' work I did on the Bill . . .

The judge: I really don't think we want to go into that.

Jenkins (beaming): I am so sorry, my Lord.

Sorry or not, the point had been made.

Against the 35 witnesses called by the defence, the prosecution brought not one. In a masterful summing up, Mr Gerald Gardiner submitted that the book would not deprave or corrupt anyone in real life, neither young people nor, 'with deference to my friend I should add, not even your wives or servants'. Members of the jury smiled at that — and at 2.35 pm on the last day of the trial they found in favour of Penguin Books, returning a verdict of not guilty.

It was never quite clear whether the jury had judged that the book was not obscene, or that it *was* obscene but redeemed by artistic merit. What is certain is that the verdict revolutionized views on what was fit to publish — and helped in a new era of permissiveness in society.

A Perfectly Ordinary Little Case

Mr Mervyn Griffith-Jones, prosecutor at the *Lady Chatterley* trial, has been immortalized for asking jury members whether they would 'wish your wife or servants to read it?' But he is almost as well remembered for another splendid utterance in a different trial. 'It is a perfectly ordinary little case of a man charged with indecency with four or five guardsmen,' he said.

'This monstrous campaign' MARIE STOPES

A hundred years ago, the subject of birth control was taboo. In Victorian novels, for example, you might come across discreet allusions to sexual activity; you might read of children born out of wedlock. But you could plough through a whole fiction library without discovering that unwanted pregnancies were preventable. This was remarkable, since overpopulation had long been considered a pressing problem, and forms of contraception had been accessible to the public since 1823. The fact was that talking about the issue was not considered very nice. Good heavens, the *ladies* might overhear.

In the event, it was the ladies who broke the silence. There was Annie Besant, tried and acquitted in 1877 on an immorality charge for publishing a family planning tract. There was Margaret Sanger, who first coined the term 'birth control' in her magazine *The Woman Rebel*, in 1914. And then there was Dr Marie Stopes.

Born in 1880, Marie Charlotte Carmichael Stopes was a quite extra-ordinary woman. Energetic, intelligent and compassionate, she also managed to be wilful, humourless and entirely lacking in tact. She had worked as a botanist at Manchester University until the failure of her first marriage in 1916 started her thinking about marital problems. Two years later she published her notorious *Married Love* — a study of happiness in married couples.

It was not primarily a book about sex or birth control. But since the subjects were germane to her theme she weighed in with confidence. Sex, she argued, should not just be something for men to enjoy; women should also take pleasure in it to the benefit of a loving marriage. The reason why women often failed to find happiness was through fear of unwanted pregnancies. And so she advocated contraception.

Outrage! *The Times* refused to carry advertisements for the book, which proved a marvellous publicity boost. Over 2,000 copies were sold in a fortnight and the volume swiftly ran through a phenomenal 26 editions. Marie Stopes used the proceeds to set up a birth-control clinic, which opened at Holloway in north London in March 1921. There, a fully qualified nursing staff gave free advice and fitting of contraceptives to poor mothers. The favoured method was the rubber check pessary — issued at cost price.

The clinic proved a roaring success among the careworn women of London's teeming slums. But many leading churchmen and doctors took exception to Marie Stopes's crusade. In particular, a Dr Halliday

Dr Marie Stopes at home

Gibson Sutherland from Edinburgh University decided to take up cudgels; learning that a certain Professor McIlroy considered the check pessary dangerous, and being a devout Catholic, Sutherland produced his own book on the subject of birth control. The publication contained provocative passages about Marie Stopes. Sutherland complained of 'exposing the poor to experiment', and wrote:

'In the midst of a London slum, a woman who is a Doctor of *German* Philosophy has opened a birth control clinic where women are instructed in a method of contraception described by Professor McIlroy as "the most harmful method of which I have had experience". It is truly amazing that this monstrous campaign should be tolerated by the Home Secretary.'

Dauntlessly, Marie Stopes took up the challenge, suing Sutherland for libel and defamation of character.

The 9-day trial opened at the High Court on 21 February 1921, and battalions of distinguished medics were conscripted as witnesses by both sides. In the end, the conflicting medical evidence probably nullified itself, but there were some heated exchanges with the Bench. The presiding judge, through his interventions, came down clearly on the side of Halliday Sutherland and exhibited an obvious distaste for the whole subject.

'What possible good would it do to young persons to learn about check pessaries?' he fumed at a witness at one point.

Dr Meredith Young, for Marie Stopes, replied, 'If they do not learn it in a cleanly and proper manner, they will learn it in a dirty and sordid manner.'

'Why should they?' the Lord Chief Justice persisted, and embarked on a diatribe to the effect that millions of people breeze serenely through life without knowing the first thing about these blasted check pessaries. In a case bristling with gynaecological talk, his exasperation was perhaps understandable. But it was a male exasperation — these things were women's matters of no concern to a gentleman. And that, in a sense, was the point: unwanted pregnancies might be of no concern to gentlemen but they were of intimate concern to the mothers involved.

Marie Stopes herself counterpoised 'wise scientific prevention' with the 'horrible criminal abortion' so frequently practised in slumland. *Experimenting* on the poor? But the rubber pessary had been in use for more than 40 years — what was experimental about it? And in the end she received a mixed verdict from the all-male jury. After deliberating for four hours, they decided that the libel was substantially true but that it did not amount to fair comment, and £100 damages were awarded to her.

Marie Stopes subsequently won a full victory in the Appeal Court — but lost when Dr Sutherland took his case on to the House of Lords. Ordered to return the damages and repay very substantial costs, she ended up legally and financially the loser. But Marie Stopes had won a prize far more valuable in terms of mass publicity. The great taboo had been lifted — and lifted definitively.

The Monkey trial

JOHN T. SCOPES

Not long ago the great 'Monkey Trial' of 1925 seemed no more than a quirk of history. Darwin's theory of evolution was so widely accepted that it seemed preposterous that anyone could have been tried in a US court for teaching it. Today, with a revival of Fundamentalist preaching about human origins, Darwin's supporters have been forced again on to the defensive in the United States and elsewhere. The issues fought out in that Tennessee courtroom have quickened once more.

The classic encounter had its origins in March 1925, when a Bill was passed in Tennessee prohibiting the teaching of evolution in any of the state's schools. In fact, any theory which denied the divine creation of man, as described in the Bible, was supposed to be banned. John Thomas Scopes, a biology teacher in Rhea High School, Dayton, carefully considered the legislation and decided, with his principal's backing, that he would continue to teach evolution as he had always done, using the standard *Hunter's Civic Biology* as his textbook. He was duly arrested and brought to trial.

The Dayton courtroom became a showcase for the talents of Clarence Darrow, the most famous lawyer in America and a man already legendary in his lifetime. He had made his name defending labour leaders but had more recently turned to criminal cases and was defence counsel in the sensational trial of the young killers Leopold and Loeb (see page 25). At 68, Darrow was still in his prime, and relished the forthcoming encounter. He had, in fact, asked for the job of defending Scopes: 'For the first, the last, the only time in my life I volunteered my services in a case. I did this because I really wanted to take part in it.'

Facing him in the Dayton court was the famous politician and orator William Jennings Bryan. Three times a candidate for the Presidency and Secretary of State under Woodrow Wilson, Bryan was a passionate believer in the literal truth of the Bible and a champion of the Fundamentalist cause. He went to Dayton to help in the prosecution, and with the eyes of the nation upon the proceedings, he became in effect the chief prosecutor.

The trial opened on 10 July and lasted for two weeks. Judge Raulston, presiding, dealt Darrow a blow by refusing to permit his many scientific experts and their testimony to be heard. Neither religion nor evolution, said the judge, was on trial — the defendant had been indicted for violating a specific state law. But the argument cut both ways and Darrow saw to it that Bryan was also prevented from delivering the long speech he had prepared to refute evolutionary theory.

In fact, the highlight of the trial was a devastating cross-examination by Darrow, questioning Bryan on the literal truth of the Bible. Did Bryan really believe that Joshua made the sun stand still? Bryan replied that he believed what the Bible said. But surely, Darrow continued, the sun *did* stand still — it was the earth that moved around it.

Darrow: Now, Mr Bryan, have you ever pondered what would have happened to the earth if it stood still suddenly?

Bryan: No.

Darrow: Don't you know it would have been converted into a molten mass of matter?

Darrow repeatedly taxed his opponent on the findings of modern scholarship. He asked, for example, how long ago Bryan thought the Flood had occurred. 'Two thousand three hundred and forty-eight years BC,' replied the Fundamentalist. Darrow pointed out that the ancient civilizations of China and Egypt had existed for thousands of years before that. Did Bryan really have not the least curiosity about such discrepancies? 'Where have you lived all your life?' Darrow asked. 'Not near you,' replied Bryan hotly.

On the biblical account of human origins, Bryan was equally stubborn.

Darrow: Mr Bryan, do you believe that the first woman was Eve?
Bryan: Yes.
Darrow: Do you believe she was literally made out of Adam's rib?
Bryan: I do.
Darrow: Did you ever discover where Cain got his wife?
Bryan: No, sir; I leave the agnostics to hunt for her.

Almost playfully, Darrow concluded by asking whether Bryan honestly believed that snakes slithered along the ground as punishment for the part played by their ancestor in the Garden of Eden.

Darrow: Do you think that is why the serpent is compelled to crawl upon its belly?
Bryan: I believe that.
Darrow: Have you any idea how the snake went about before that time?
Bryan: No, sir.
Darrow: Do you know whether he walked on his tail or not?
Bryan: No, sir, I have no way to know.

The Fundamentalists were humiliated. On 21 July, Scopes was found guilty and fined $100, but that was scarcely important. Darrow in fact *asked* for a verdict of guilty so that the case could be taken on appeal to Tennessee's Supreme Court — where Scopes was to win on a technicality, without any expression of opinion being given as to whether the law was constitutional or not.

Dayton had staged the grand encounter, and the moral victory was entirely Darrow's. It can however have given him no pleasure to learn that his eminent opponent was taken ill on the last day of the Dayton trial — the unhappy Bryan died only five days later.

Not Naughty Enough

Times have changed since the *Lady Chatterley* trial. In May 1984, a 26-year-old Sussex plumber filed a complaint against a local sex-shop, claiming that five pornographic videos he had hired to view with his ex-wife were not explicit enough. The court at Worthing found in his favour, awarding a £15 refund. After the hearing the plumber said, 'I think I have proved the point that these shops cannot get away with taking customers for a ride simply because they are too embarrassed to complain.'

'One sorry lifetime'

CARYL CHESSMAN

Amid all the tortuous legal wranglings over the fate of Caryl Chessman, two questions stood out clearly. Was he the Red Light Bandit? And if so, should he die?

Caryl Chessman was 27 when the case opened in California. In the space of three days, someone had held up two young women in their cars and led them at gunpoint to his own vehicle where he made them perform oral sex. The man was dubbed the 'Red Light Bandit' because of a flashing red light on his car, and Chessman, who had been in trouble with the law from childhood, was accused of the offences.

All sex crimes are ugly and the ordeal of the victims was no doubt terrifying. But Caryl Chessman was not accused of a sexual offence; incredibly, he was charged with kidnapping his two victims with intent to rob with bodily harm. Kidnapping in the state of California carried the capital penalty and, convicted by a Los Angeles jury in July 1948, Chessman was sentenced to death.

There were appeals. For one thing, Chessman protested his innocence, claiming that he had not been properly identified by the victims. Then there were irregularities in the procedure: Chessman alleged that he was denied access to law books and other proper opportunities to conduct his defence. One particularly serious allegation made by the convicted man was that passages in the transcription of his first trial had been forged (the court reporter had died before completing his notes).

But above all, Chessman's case became notorious because of the preposterous kidnapping charge. California had introduced the death penalty for kidnapping in the wake of the famous Lindbergh case (when the child of the great aviator was abducted). The death penalty was supposed to cover cases where a ransom was asked and the kidnap victim suffered bodily harm. How could Chessman's case be described in that category? After making his victims endure forced sex, the Red Light Bandit had released them without further physical injury. The capital charge was only invoked on the shaky pretexts that the bandit drove one of his victims a short distance in his car (hence it was a kidnapping) and he had taken $5 from the other (hence it was kidnapping with robbery). In short, it looked as if the kidnapping charge had been invoked *in order* that the culprit might die.

Chessman's appeals dragged on for almost 12 years after his initial conviction. The Korean war came and went; Rock 'n' Roll swept the

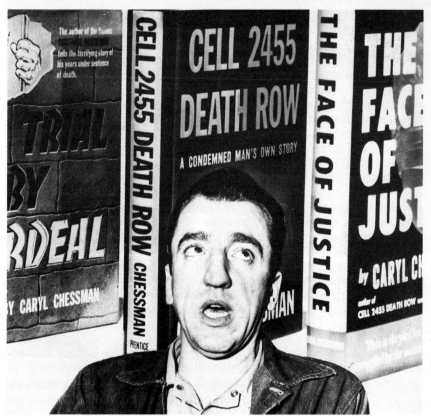

Chessman against his three best selling books

nation; the first satellites were launched, and the Swinging Sixties opened. Through all that time Caryl Chessman waited in San Quentin on Death Row: by the end he had filed no fewer than 50 appeals to various courts — and survived no fewer than nine execution dates. While under the shadow of death he educated himself in the prison library and became an entirely changed character: all who met him spoke of his dignity and humanity. Chessman even wrote a best-seller, *Cell 2455 Death Row,* about the ordeal of waiting, and a *Ballad of Caryl Chessman* was released on disc to become a hit record.

By the spring of 1960, Chessman had won the ultimate American accolade by appearing on the cover of *Time* magazine. And his cause had a following worldwide. The issue of capital punishment was being passionately debated on both sides of the Atlantic and Chessman seemed to symbolize all the moral ambiguities of judicial killing. What purpose would it serve society to gas this humane and intelligent man?

Suppose he *was* the Red Light Bandit — had he not expiated his guilt by now?

Within the United States, the death penalty had already been abolished by nine states, and California's Governor Brown was among those who wanted to see its end. When Chessman's final execution date was set, the Governor ordered a 60-day stay of execution so that voting on capital punishment could take place in the Californian senate. But the Bill for abolition was kept off the Senate floor by its opponents, and time was at last running out.

Chessman's last appeal to the Supreme Court was based on the grounds that 12 years in a death cell constituted a 'cruel and unusual punishment', thereby violating his constitutional rights. It failed. The date for execution had been set at 2 May 1960, and on the night beforehand protest groups started gathering outside the state penitentiary; among those present was the young film star Marlon Brando. Pleas for clemency were meanwhile flooding into the office of Governor Brown from figures as disparate as Brigitte Bardot, Dr Albert Schweitzer and the cellist Pablo Casals. And right up to the last minute, it was uncertain whether the execution would really go ahead.

In Washington, Justice William Douglas rejected one last-ditch attempt to save Chessman. Just 12 minutes before the execution time, the Californian Supreme Court denied a stay of execution by a vote of only 4 to 3.

The final desperate irony occurred in San Francisco, where a federal judge was preparing to grant a 30–minute stay of execution so that yet another plea from one of Chessman's lawyers could be heard. The judge told his secretary to phone San Quentin; the secretary dialled the wrong number. By the time the judge did get through the execution had already begun.

Caryl Chessman died at 10 am Pacific Daylight Time in the gas chamber at San Quentin. The crowds outside wept or prayed at the fatal moment, and newspaper editorials throughout the world expressed revulsion the following day.

Before his death, the condemned man had drawn up a number of statements which were now released for publication. He reiterated his innocence, claiming that 'in my lifetime I was guilty of many crimes, but not those for which my life was taken'. He wrote of the 'senseless tragedy and witless futility' of capital punishment, and hoped that society would soon have the courage and the vision to eliminate it. Chessman expressed the final hope that his supporters would continue to speak out against 'gas chambers and executioners and retributive justice'.

In conclusion, he wrote, 'You ask me about a future life. I believe there is none. Caryl Chessman has gone to oblivion so that society can forget one sorry lifetime.'

Legacy of error

THE THALIDOMIDE CASE

The drug was developed by a German chemical firm in the late 1950s, and sold internationally under at least 50 different names. In Britain it appeared as 'Distaval', 'Tensival' or 'Asmaval'. Essentially, it was billed as a completely safe sedative and sleeping pill — something rather miraculous because, unlike barbiturates, it had no toxic side effects — and it was commonly prescribed by doctors to deal with tension in expectant mothers.

The name of the drug was thalidomide.

We know today that the early claims made for it were tragically wrong, and that the legacy of error was horrific. If taken between the fourth and sixth weeks of pregnancy, when a foetus forms its limbs, thalidomide created an almost even chance of deformity in the child. Some babies were born without arms, some without legs and some were born without either. Internationally, between 1959 and 1962, some 8,000 children came into the world deformed.

Claims for compensation were lodged worldwide. In Britain, perhaps 400 children had suffered and the drug was withdrawn from the market in November 1961. It was exactly a year later that the first British family issued a writ against the firm who had made and sold thalidomide in Britain: Distillers Co. (Biochemicals) Ltd, a subsidiary of the multi-million pound liquor group, Distillers.

In the period that followed, 61 children brought actions through their parents against the company, alleging negligence and seeking compensation. But it was not until 1967 that the cases approached trial. Distillers then offered to settle out of court — so long as the allegations of negligence were dropped. The parents agreed, having been advised that their cause presented twofold difficulties. For one thing, a foetus was not at that time a 'person' in the eyes of the law; for another, proving negligence would be an incredibly long and costly business. And of course, if the parents failed to prove their cases, they would not get a penny in damages.

So it suited everyone to make an out-of-court settlement. The problem was, how much should be paid? How did you put a price on the suffering of the families, the maimed futures of 60-odd children? Despite the parents' agreement, the lawyers could not fix the sum to be paid, so two of the deformed children were taken before the High Court as test cases. As a result of this move, Distillers agreed to pay a total of roughly £1 million to the children involved.

Afterwards, many more parents tried to take legal action and the number of thalidomide children represented rose to over 300. In 1971, Distillers suggested a new proposal whereby a charitable trust would be set up for the victims, receiving £3.25 million over ten years. But there was a catch: *all* the parents must agree to the offer — there could be no maverick claims.

Most of the parents agreed; but six families refused, believing the compensation to be quite inadequate. Moreover, the trust would be a charity, so no claim would be enforceable by law. The whole affair took a particularly sorry turn when the majority of the parents, through their solicitors, took the six maverick families to court, asking that they be represented in the case by an Official Solicitor, on the grounds that they were not acting in their children's best interests.

The High Court decided against the group of six; but five of them went on to win in the Court of Appeal. Distillers then slightly revised their offer and excluded the insistence on total agreement among parents.

By now it was 1972 — ten years since the first writ was issued. Yet the case was so shackled by legal constraints on media coverage that the general public was barely aware of the plight of the thalidomide children and their parents. Deadpan reports of the complex situation certainly appeared — but comment was minimal because of editorial fears of contempt of court.

It was the *Sunday Times* that broke the silence, under its editor Harold Evans. Outraged by the families' situation, he decided to campaign strongly and openly on their behalf — at risk of clashing with the law if necessary.

On 24 September 1972, the crusade opened with a forthright editorial and an extended article headed 'Our Thalidomide Children — A Cause for National Shame'. The paper attacked the existing state of law which compounded human tragedies with lengthy court battles. It attacked the government for failing to open an inquiry into the drug disaster of thalidomide. And it attacked Distillers, too. 'No money can ever compensate for being born a limbless trunk, but at least a generous compensation can give the glimmer of a normal life.' It was in generosity that Distillers had failed: 'It is appreciated that Distillers' lawyers have a professional duty to secure the best terms for their clients. But at the end of the day, what is to be paid in settlement is the decision of Distillers and they should offer much, much more to every one of the thalidomide victims.'

In addition to exploring the existing position, the *Sunday Times* also announced that it would shortly be publishing a long investigation into the original cause of the tragedy.

The campaign rolled in the weeks that followed, gaining momentum in other newspapers, radio and television. And the effects of the furore were dramatic. In 1973, Distillers submitted a new offer of £20 million — about 7 times as much as their original one. The settlement was almost unanimously accepted by the parents, approved in the High Court and commended by the *Sunday Times* itself.

The affair did not end there, however. Controversy was to rage about the administration of the trust fund and its investments; about whether payments should be exempt from tax; and about the so-called Y List of over a hundred cases in which it was not agreed that deformations were caused by thalidomide. Meanwhile, the thalidomide children were ceasing to be children; stories of their human courage and resilience featured repeatedly in the press — of the first victim to get a job and the first to pass a driving test. In 1978 an armless thalidomide victim gave birth to a daughter; in 1979 a thalidomide youth won a karate belt.

But the case had also raised important legal issues. The *Sunday Times* had been restrained from publishing its promised investigation into the causes of the disaster, on the grounds that it might prejudice the outcome of legal claims against Distillers. After battles in the Divisional Court and the Appeal Court, the case went to the House of Lords, where five Law Lords ruled unanimously that the article's publication must be postponed until all claims had been resolved.

Two conflicting public interests were exposed: Distillers' right to a fair hearing against the *Sunday Times*'s right of press freedom. The newspaper took its case to the EEC Commission of Human Rights, which in 1977 ruled that the ban on publication was wrong; five years after the article was due to appear its release was at last permitted. In 1979, the European Court at Strasbourg ruled that the ban had violated human rights — and in the same year Harold Evans was awarded a gold medal for his campaign against the injunction.

No, Minister CLIVE PONTING

At 7 pm on 2 May 1982, Argentina's second largest warship, the 13,645-ton *General Belgrano* was torpedoed by the nuclear-powered HMS *Conqueror*, one of Britain's hunter-killer submarines. The aged Argentine cruiser — a veteran of Pearl Harbor — sank into the icy waters of the South Atlantic, and with her died 368 men.

It was the first major loss of life in the Falklands conflict, an event of terrible significance. Horror and consternation were expressed worldwide, even by foreign governments which supported Britain in the dispute. And the event prompted a swift Argentine response in the sinking by Exocet missile of the British destroyer HMS *Sheffield*. Suddenly, hopes of a negotiated settlement seemed to vanish into thin air. It was going to be a shooting war.

Why was the *Belgrano* attacked in the first place? As Britain's task force made its way towards the invaded islands, a 200-mile total exclusion zone was established around them, with a warning that any foreign vessels penetrating the zone were at risk. But the *General Belgrano* was in fact outside the zone when hit, and the government's critics were not satisfied by vague assurances that the warship posed a threat to the task force. Some even suggested that the *Belgrano* was torpedoed quite cynically, in order to scotch a Peruvian peace plan which was under consideration.

Whatever the truth, it is certain that the official version of the sinking, as given at the time and in the subsequent government White Paper on the Falklands, contained certain omissions and errors of fact. For example, the White Paper stated clearly that the *Belgrano* was detected on 2 May — the day of the sinking. But the captain of HMS *Conqueror* afterwards said in an interview that the warship was first detected on 1 May — the day beforehand — and Mrs Thatcher subsequently confirmed his disclosure.

Again, the official version referred to the warship 'sailing near to the total exclusion zone'. It did not mention that the *Belgrano* had in fact reversed course, and was heading westward away from it.

Long after the war was over, questions continued to be fired in parliament about the *Belgrano* issue; the government was put under pressure and, at the Ministry of Defence, it was the job of a talented young assistant secretary to draft replies to letters and questions. His name was Clive Ponting.

Aged 38, Clive Ponting was one of the closest advisers to Michael Heseltine, Secretary of State for Defence after the Falklands War. For his minister Ponting prepared a definitive narrative of the sinking of the *Belgrano*, a document so sensitive that it came to be known as the 'Crown Jewels' among his fellow civil servants. Ponting was in no way a radical as far as the incident was concerned. He did not believe that the government had anything sinister to hide; never did he suggest that the warship was sunk for any reason other than that it threatened the task force. But when the government came under pressure, he believed, ministers misled parliament about the incident and were planning to mislead a select committee of the House of Commons too. Where did his duty lie; in loyalty to the government, or to parliament? Ponting decided in favour of the latter and he sent, anonymously, two documents to the Labour MP Tam Dalyell, a well-known critic of the

Belgrano sinking. (The documents were not classified: one was a draft of replies to questions by Tam Dalyell on the *Belgrano* incident; the other was a paper on how to handle questions from the Commons select committee.)

When the leak was discovered, Ponting came under suspicion and confessed to his superiors. He offered his resignation — but it was not accepted. Instead, a decision was taken to prosecute him under Section 2 of the Official Secrets Act.

What had begun as an issue about the *Belgrano* now became a much wider debate on government secrecy and freedom of information. Whitehall's tradition of silence was notorious, and viewers of TV's popular series *Yes, Minister* were familiar with the atmosphere of cosy conspiracy in which civil servants appeared to operate. Ponting represented a challenge to that tradition.

The trial opened at the Central Criminal Court on 28 January 1985. Ponting pleaded not guilty to breaching the Official Secrets Act, so challenging the prosecution to show how he had failed in his duty as a civil servant. On the very first day, his counsel took the offensive, saying, 'This is not a case about spying. It is a case about lying or misleading parliament.'

The prosecution agreed that there was no question of national security being at risk in Ponting's actions. But it alleged that he had breached confidentiality by passing documents to an unauthorized person.

The trial lasted for two weeks and was followed with fascination nationwide. Channel 4 proposed televising nightly dramatized versions of the proceedings; the judge banned the proposal, but court transcripts were permitted to be televised using newsreaders instead of actors. And there were some moments of real-life drama in the court itself. The MP Tam Dalyell was himself present for much of the trial, and was at one point ordered to come before the bench. The judge warned him that he had been making remarks about the trial outside the courtroom which might influence the jury within. These must cease. Dalyell replied with spirit and after heated exchanges the judge concluded by warning him that he risked gaol if he continued to make statements on matters *sub judice*: 'If you cannot control yourself for another week, even after this warning, I may be driven to put you where you will have no option.'

Mr Dalyell took the hint. He made no further remarks for the duration.

Several eminent figures testified on Ponting's behalf, and his character emerged unblemished from the trial. It was even learned that, by an irony, Mrs Thatcher herself had intervened to make sure that he was given a senior post in the Ministry of Defence. His political views were middle of the road; he had enjoyed his work in the civil service. It just happened that he was one of the few people in the Ministry to know all the facts surrounding the sinking, and felt it was his responsibility to act. 'The ministers were sending to parliament a document that was misleading and deliberately misleading,' he said.

At the heart of the debate was the Official Secrets Act, framed in 1911 and widely regarded as repressive in spirit. But it is also vague in certain key areas. One important passage, for example, describes communicating information as an offence, unless 'it is in the interests of the state (a person's) duty to communicate it'. The thrust of Ponting's defence was that it was in the interests of the state that the truth be told to the House of Commons. He had made a very limited disclosure in the belief that there could be no breach of the Act if unclassified information were given to the House: 'Either information is classified and cannot be released; or unclassified and can.' In cross-examination he was asked, was it not up to the Secretary of State for Defence to decide where to draw the line? Not, replied Ponting, 'where he is attempting to cover up information which might be politically embarrassing'. Ponting declared that parliament was being fed 'highly slanted material which suggested they did not need to go any further with their enquiries'.

In their *summings up*, the counsels presented diametrically opposed views. The defence stated that civil servants should not blindly follow confidentiality; the prosecution said that leaks were bound to undermine the governing process. And on the tenth day, the judge summed up strongly in favour of the prosecution on points of law. He declared that the 'interests of state' were the same as government policy: 'The Government policy, rightly or wrongly, was to give no further information on the *Belgrano*.' The jury should avoid questions of sympathy for Mr Ponting, his good character or their own political beliefs; the *Belgrano* leak was against the interests of state.

The result of the trial now looked like a foregone conclusion. Ponting's solicitor was to say that, after the judge's summing up, he rated the chances of acquittal at about 300-1. It was reported too that at one point in the trial, when the jury was absent, the judge had told counsel that he was considering halting the proceedings and giving a direction to convict Mr Ponting.

And yet, when the jury returned after three hours, they brought in a verdict of not guilty. The foreman's announcement was greeted by cheers and applause in the courtroom. A delighted Clive Ponting smiled broadly for reporters and admitted that the verdict came to him as 'a tremendous surprise'. But it was a triumph: 'I did what I did because it was the right thing to do. Despite all the pressures, 12 ordinary people have supported that decision.'

Campaigners for greater freedom of information hailed the verdict as a devastating defeat for the Official Secrets Act. Opposition spokesmen

Clive Ponting arriving at the Old Bailey

demanded the resignation of the ministers who, on the given evidence, had been 'manoeuvring to deceive parliament'. The government and its supporters were reported to be deeply angered by the jury's decision, and a furious row erupted in parliament when Mr Kinnock, Leader of the Opposition, suggested that it had been Mrs Thatcher's decision to prosecute Ponting in the first place. Mrs Thatcher denied it; Mr Kinnock said he did not believe her; Mrs Thatcher professed outrage and demanded an apology . . . a flurry of letters were passed between the two, some (to the delight of political cartoonists) on St Valentine's Day.

The controversy did not end there. It was revealed that one of the jurors, a Ms Lynne Oliver, was a Labour councillor for Islington and had previously voted at a council meeting for the withdrawal of charges against Mr Ponting. Could she be described as impartial?

But the disclosure did not really diminish the impact of the verdict. The whole jury — eight men and four women — had listened to the evidence, heard the judge's directions, and made up their own minds. Their decision transcended the legal niceties and they had acted in what *The Times* leader called 'sublime disregard for the oppressive spirit which formulated Section 2 of the Official Secrets Act'. A cartoon on the newspaper's front page expressed a similar view more succinctly. The caption read simply, 'Not guilty — *so there!*'

CHAPTER 5

Society Scandals

Claus Von Bülow
Elizabeth Chudleigh
The Tichborne Claimant
Stephen Ward

Deacon Brodie
Sir William Gordon-Cumming
Oscar Wilde

The sleeping beauty case CLAUS VON BÜLOW

It ran for almost five years as America's grand real-life soap opera. And money — incredible amounts of money — played the lead role. Danish-born socialite Claus von Bülow was accused of trying to murder his wife Martha by twice injecting her with insulin. The alleged motive? The $14 million share he could expect from her $75 million fortune.

This was big, big money — even by the standards of Newport, Rhode Island, the fashionable summer resort of multi-millionaires where the couple had lived in their palatial mansion. But Martha von Bülow lived there no more. From December 1980, 'Sunny' (as she was known) had been in coma in a New York hospital, cared for at a cost of $500,000 a year. Every few hours her inert body was turned over to guard against bed sores; otherwise she was practically motionless and the doctors considered her condition irreversible. Almost no-one believed she would ever recover: no-one, that is, except her eldest son Alexander and her daughter Annie, who played tapes of Sunny's favourite music by her bedside in the hope that one day she would wake up.

That son and daughter — von Bülow's stepchildren — were the socialite's chief accusers (von Bülow's own daughter by the marriage stood by him through his trials). The stepchildren alleged that the present coma, and one a year earlier, were caused by injections administered by von Bülow from a 'little black bag' of needles and insulin which he was said to have possessed. Not only had he wanted his share of the fortune, they claimed, but he also wanted to marry his mistress Alexandra Isles.

Von Bülow replied that the comas resulted from his wife's over-indulgence in barbiturate drugs and alcohol — and the media went wild. Here were sex, drink, drugs, an alleged murder attempt, the supposed victim in coma — all set against a multi-million dollar back-drop that made TV's *Dallas* seem cheap by comparison. When von Bülow's first trial was televised, millions of Americans got to know and love or hate the central cast of characters in what was billed as 'The Sleeping Beauty Case'. Above all, they got familiar with von Bülow himself: suave, elegant and faintly sardonic, the perfect image of a European gentleman, who spoke with traces of a classy English accent picked up during years spent in London.

Did he do it?

At the first trial, which ended at Newport in 1982, the jury decided that he did. The key witness was the comatose woman's maid, Maria Schralhammer, who had found the insulin and needles in Claus's closet and asked 'Insulin? For what insulin?' Found guilty, Claus von Bülow was sentenced to 30 years' imprisonment. But he never went to gaol, for the conviction was overturned on a legal technicality. And with the deepening fascination of the American public, the case went to a second trial.

The new proceedings opened at Providence, Rhode Island, in April 1985. So much had now been written about the whole affair that it was a daunting task to find an impartial jury. Even when one was agreed its members had to be locked up in a hotel at night, forbidden to read newspapers, watch TV or listen to the radio. Indeed, they were not even permitted to hear all of the discussions about legal technicalities in case they should be prejudiced — during one three-day period they were in court for only three hours.

This cocoon of secrecy, though, freed the media completely from any restraint. Since the jury could not, supposedly, be influenced, practically anything went. The whole two-month trial was carried live on cable television, and commentators weighed up the odds for and against conviction almost as if assessing a snooker match. In Providence itself, local radio stations took polls and sweepstakes on the outcome. Even as the jury retired to consider the verdict that would determine his fate, von Bülow spoke to reporters. He and his new girlfriend publicly predicted a hung jury, on the grounds that its members would probably want to keep the soap opera going. 'I am not up on a charge of adultery,' he reflected. 'They are not judging me on whether I was a nice fellow. They are judging me on whether there was a crime.'

Within the courtroom, much of the evidence from the first trial was brought up again. The judge even insisted that Alexandra Isles return from Europe to testify as she had done before. (In the earlier trial, von Bülow's former mistress had alleged that, in 1979, von Bülow wanted the money to marry her.) There were moments of high emotion in this as in the earlier trial, with witnesses choking back tears and members of the jury clearly overcome too.

But in certain key areas, Judge Corrine P. Grande admitted less evidence than before. In particular, the jury was barred from hearing facts about Mrs von Bülow's will and what her husband might expect from it. The possibility of a financial motive was diminished and this removed a weighty plank from the prosecution's platform.

Marc DeSisto, the young state prosecutor, certainly gave the case all he had got, resorting to studied theatricals in evoking key episodes from the case. In treating the alleged crime, for example, he harnessed near sexual imagery: 'He's pressing the plunger in, the insulin is in her body. . . . Imagine the relief from tension he feels.' Von Bülow endured the performance almost impassively, eyes closed, with fingers to his cheeks. In neither trial did he choose to enter the witness box.

Defence attorney Thomas Puccio, though, made his case with terrific force. He relied almost exclusively on the evidence of nine medical experts for the defence who testified that Mrs von Bülow's death could not be attributed to insulin. 'No insulin injection!' Puccio hammered his point incessantly at the jury: 'No insulin injection!' It was an insistent, unflamboyant but very powerful theme. If there was no insulin injection, where was the crime?

On Monday, 10 June 1985, after 12 hours of deliberation, the jury returned to the courtroom. The TV cameras focused on von Bülow's taut features as one, then the other murder charge was read out. On the first charge he was found not guilty, and a premature wave of exultation seemed about to break from his supporters in the gallery. Von Bülow, though, had remembered the second charge and was framed in an agony of tension. Then came the second, 'Not guilty'. He buckled as if shocked with electricity, and momentarily covered his face. Then he smiled; then he cried. His supporters started cheering.

Claus von Bülow walked from the court a free man and spoke outside to the press. Drawing deeply on a cigarette, he said that the result had ended five years of worry. Asked about his plans, he said that he intended to lead a quiet life, 'and to give up smoking'. Later — and fittingly in a case so saturated by media interest — he gave a televised press conference with his lawyers. He said that he had no hard feelings towards his stepchildren, and declared that he would have liked to give evidence himself, but added, 'this was conducted quite rightly as a medical case. There was no crime.'

A contemplative Claus Von Bulow

The stepchildren themselves also spoke to the press and declared themselves unhappy with the verdict. It was predicted that legal battles would ensue over the $75 million fortune. At the time of writing, Martha 'Sunny' von Bülow was still lying senseless in her New York hospital, mute subject of one of the most sensational cases in the annals of US law.

The real Dr Jekyll

DEACON BRODIE

He has become one of fiction's immortals: Dr Jekyll, the respected scientist, who turns by night into a monster of depravity. Robert Louis Stevenson was inspired to write the tale by a drug-induced nightmare. But the theme of duality had possessed him since his early childhood when his nurse used to tell him stories about a real-life villain named William Brodie who had haunted the lamp-lit streets of Edinburgh a hundred years before.

Like the fictional Dr Jekyll, Brodie seemed on the outside to be a pillar of the establishment. Like Dr Jekyll he was driven to the dark excitement of a lurid underworld. In Stevenson's childhood bedroom there stood a large mahogany cupboard said to have been made by Brodie himself. And only four years before he published his *The Strange Case of Dr Jekyll and Mr Hyde* (1886), Stevenson had collaborated with W. E. Henley to write a stage play called *Deacon Brodie or the Double Life*.

Born in 1741, William Brodie was the son of a prosperous cabinet-maker and, by the age of 40, had risen to become Deacon, or head, of the cabinet-makers' guild. He was also a city councillor and a man of considerable influence. But Brodie had a secret life too: a bachelor, he kept two separate mistresses and supported five illegitimate children. He gambled on cards, dice and the gamecocks that fought out their bloody duels in the seedy Grassmarket cockpit. And Brodie's misdeeds extended far beyond the province of such 'gentlemanly' vices as gambling and wenching. For the Deacon was also behind the spate of robberies that began suddenly in Edinburgh in the summer of 1786.

They started one night in August when, using a skeleton key, someone opened the bank door at the Royal Exchange and made off with £800 sterling. There followed a wave of break-ins at fashionable shops. Even Edinburgh's famous University was not safe: a 300-year-old silver mace went missing from the College Library. The depredations continued until, on the evening of 8 March 1788, the mystery gang attempted its most daring stroke — and made its first great mistake.

That night, a lawyer named James Bonar was returning to collect some papers from the General Excise Office — headquarters of Scotland's Customs and Excise. As he tried the front door, a man in black coat and black hat burst from the passage and disappeared into the shadows. Not long after, a whistle was blown in the street by some watching confederate and two more figures flitted from the house to vanish into the night. Mr Bonar had interrupted a burglary.

The bungled break-in was the talk of all Edinburgh the next day, and it was to spell Brodie's doom. Not long afterwards, John Brown, one of the thieves, turned King's Evidence in exchange for the offer of a pardon. He named two of his accomplices — Ainslie and Smith — and also told the authorities that one of the town's leading citizens was involved. Realizing that the net was closing in, Brodie fled by post-chaise to London, and from there by sloop to Ostend. In his absence, a £200 reward was offered for information leading to his arrest, and George Smith made a confession.

Brodie was eventually tracked down to Amsterdam, where he was found hiding in a cupboard at an alehouse while awaiting a passage to New York. Once he had been properly identified he was extradited and brought back to Edinburgh to face trial with George Smith on a charge of armed robbery at the Excise Office.

The trial opened at the Parliament House in August 1788. Its sensational aspects had guaranteed packed public benches, and the presiding judge, Lord Braxfield, was perhaps the most famous in the history of Scottish criminal law. All the cards seemed stacked against Brodie as he walked into the dock, wearing a blue coat and black satin breeches. But he looked confident, and had a formidable defence counsel in Henry Erskine ('the best cock that ever fought,' Brodie called him).

The prosecution had damning evidence. For example, pistols and a dark lanthorn were found in Brodie's yard. There were the suspicious implications of his sudden flight, as well as compromising passages in some letters written on board ship. In one, for example, he described to a friend how he had hidden out with a wench in London not 500 yards from Bow Street, and seen the rewards offered for his arrest. There was a daredevil relish in the excitement of the affair: 'Were I to write to you all that has happened to me and the hairsbreadth escapes I made from a well-scented pack of bloodhounds, it would make a small volume,' he wrote. But most damning of all was the evidence offered by his former accomplices.

All three of Brodie's gang had now confessed. Smith had retracted his statement, but Ainslie and Brown were offering very full accounts in exchange for offers of freedom. And the essential drama in Brodie's trial stemmed from the question of whether their evidence was admissible. Ainslie had made his confession very late in the day, and could be said to have been tempted by offers of lenient treatment. It was Brown who had first approached the authorities — but Brown had a criminal record in England. The defence pointed out that under Scottish law, this meant that he could not give evidence. The prosecution countered by producing a royal pardon which had been granted to Brown in England. This, it was argued, wiped his slate clean and made him a fit witness after all.

A furious controversy raged in court over this issue, and the defence drew wild cheers from the public benches by attacking this 'English Pardon' as an abomination in a Scottish court. Nevertheless, the court ruled that both Ainslie and Brown were entitled to give evidence — and with that Brodie's case was lost.

The court heard how Brodie had planned the Excise Office break-in over a long period. With his cover of respectability, the Deacon had been able to visit the Office in daylight and furtively make an impression in putty of the key; the duplicate was cut at his workshop. He wore a black burglar's suit on the night of the job, and had brought an old wig of his father's for disguise. As a cunning refinement he had also brought a false clue — a rider's spur — which was left on the floor at the scene of the crime to give the impression that the job was the work of men who had ridden from afar.

Unfortunately for the thieves, they could not find the secret drawer in the cashier's desk where the revenue money was stored. They obtained only petty cash — and then were disturbed by the arrival of Mr Bonar. The gang were armed with pistols and nearly shot the lawyer, but Brodie lost his nerve and fled.

Brown's and Ainslie's stories matched, and there could really be only one verdict. The jury found William Brodie and George Smith guilty, and the judge ordered that on 1 October the two men be taken to the place of execution 'tae be hingit by the necks, by the hauns o' the Common Executioner upon the gibbet until they be deid'.

During his time in the condemned cell Brodie made light of his misfortunes, joking and playing draughts with visitors. Perhaps he had hopes of a reprieve, perhaps it was sheer bravado — or perhaps his good spirits stemmed from the fantastic project he had conceived. His last wish was that friends be allowed to remove his body straight after the hanging, so that it did not remain in gaol, tainted with infamy. This wish was granted, and Brodie walked to the scaffold on the appointed day in a smart black suit with his hair dressed and powdered. Mounting the ladder before a crowd of 40,000, he betrayed no sign of emotion. On the contrary, he seemed rather perky. This was because he had bribed the hangman to give him a short drop, and not to notice the rigid steel collar he was wearing under his fashionable neckerchief. Immediately after the drop, his body would be cut down and rushed by cart to his workshop where a doctor was waiting to revive him.

Alas for Brodie, it was not to be. The authorities noticed that the hangman's rope was too short and ordered him to lengthen it. When Brodie dropped, the collar made no difference. His neck was broken, and though friends rushed him as agreed to the hired quack, the body that they rattled over the cobbles was already a corpse.

The bigamous Countess of Bristol

ELIZABETH CHUDLEIGH

An hour before midnight on 14 August 1744, Elizabeth Chudleigh, Maid of Honour to the Princess of Wales, secretly married Augustus John Hervey, son of the Earl of Bristol. The ceremony took place at the chapel of Lainston House near Winchester, by the light of a single wax taper stuck in the hat of one of the witnesses. There were only five people present besides the couple: two male witnesses for him; two women for her; and the parson, the Reverend Thomas Amis. The affair had to be kept secret for at that time the couple had poor prospects: he was no more than a junior naval officer, and she would sacrifice her £400 annual income from her Court position if she openly lost her status as a Maid. The marriage made no financial sense — the likeliest explanation is that the two were much in love and wanted to consummate their passion legally.

Afterwards, the couple spent four days and nights together before Hervey was called to set sail for the West Indies, and Elizabeth returned to Court. Subsequently, the couple saw precious little of one another. It has been speculated that Hervey was a poor sexual performer — or that he suffered from syphilis and infected her — either way, Elizabeth's ardent feelings for him died. She lived very happily on her own at her mother's house in Conduit Street and when Hervey returned on shore leave in January 1747 she only admitted him under protest. After an episode of what amounted to legal rape, she secretly bore him a son later that year. But the child died after only a few months and the relationship was over.

Elizabeth had her life to live, and she lived it to the full. The ravishing daughter of a Devonshire colonel, Miss Chudleigh (as she was still known) was a notorious figure at Court and her favours were eagerly sought by many a noble lord. 'She breathed in an atmosphere of sighs,' it is reported. 'Every butterfly fluttered around her.' If the gossip is to be believed she was even wooed and won by George II; certainly, she made herself notorious at a masquerade in Somerset House, where she appeared as Iphigenia — virtually in the nude. 'Miss Chudleigh's dress, or rather undress, was remarkable,' wrote Mrs Elizabeth Montagu, continuing that even the other Maids of Honour (by no means maids in the strictest sense) refused to speak to her.

A Georgian Gender Bender

The Countess of Bristol may have enjoyed supreme scandal in her day. But if quantity rather than quality of bigamy is to be the standard then the West Country's Mary Hamilton far outshone her.

On 7 October 1746, this remarkable woman was tried at Taunton in Somerset for wrongfully marrying no fewer than 14 times — in each case marrying other women.

The 14th wife appeared to give evidence against her, describing how they had undergone a lawful marriage and bedded and lived together for more than three months before she suspected that her partner was another woman. The 'vilest and most deceitful practices' had, it seemed, been employed to mislead her.

The judges appear to have been uncertain about the legal sex of Mary Hamilton (alias Charles Hamilton, alias George Hamilton, alias William Hamilton), but they ruled that 'he, she, the prisoner at the bar,' was an uncommon notorious cheat and was to be gaoled for six months during which time she was to be whipped in the towns of Taunton, Glastonbury, Wells and Shepton Mallet.

Sentence was duly carried out, 'in the severity of the winter'.

Elizabeth was also rebuked by her royal mistress, who threw a shawl over her in the ballroom. But the gallant Miss Chudleigh was indifferent to all criticism and continued to behave as scandalously as ever. Practically no-one at this stage knew about her secret marriage.

Twelve years passed after the death of her child and the break with Augustus John Hervey. She turned down offers of marriage from figures as eminent as the Duke of Hamilton and the Duke of Ancaster. But a hankering for title and secure wealth seems to have stayed with her. In 1759, it was reported that the old Earl of Bristol was mortally sick. If he died, and her marriage were made public, she would become Countess of Bristol, commanding a fortune of £100,000. Elizabeth hastened to Hampshire and the aged Reverend Amis, demanding documentation of the marriage. With the aid of a lawyer, she persuaded the parson to backdate the church register to include an entry for her secret wedding.

All that she needed now was for the old Earl to die — unfortunately for her, he recovered from his illness and lived on for almost ten years more!

Elizabeth must have gnashed her teeth at this unwanted turn of events. But a more glittering prospect began to beckon. For some time she lived more or less openly as mistress to the very wealthy Duke of Kingston, a veteran of Culloden. And when the Duke offered her his hand in marriage she was ready, at last, to accept. The trouble was that the tables had turned: the secret marriage, which she had earlier been so eager to have certified, now stood in the way of her hopes.

Hervey also wanted to extricate himself from any marital obligation, and suggested a divorce in which Elizabeth should appear as the guilty party. Elizabeth was outraged and replied with a very rude letter to the effect that she refused 'to prove herself a whore' for his sake. No, on legal advice she chose a different course, deciding to sue her husband in a Church court for the offence of jactitation of marriage (falsely claiming a marriage to have taken place). The suit began in November 1768, and by February of the next year an ecclesiastical court granted a favourable decree. On 8 March 1769, Miss Elizabeth Chudleigh married the Duke of Kingston, and nobody raised any just cause or impediment.

For four years the couple lived together as man and wife, the Duchess giving lavish fêtes and balls as befitted her high position in society. And when the Duke died, childless, on 23 September 1773, she was set to inherit practically the whole of his fortune, for she had seen to it that his second will was very favourable: it left almost everything to her and nothing to the Duke's surviving sister, wife of a man named Meadows, or the Meadows children.

Meadows immediately started Chancery proceedings, claiming that the Duchess had exercised undue influence over the will. And it was during these proceedings that the questions arose: was Elizabeth really the Duchess of Kingston? Or was she the Countess of Bristol (for the old Earl had at last died)?

Formally charged with bigamy, Elizabeth came back from a trip to Europe to stand trial in the House of Lords.

Proceedings opened on 15 April 1776, at Westminster Hall, amid gorgeous pomp and ceremony. The Queen, Prince of Wales and Princess Royal were all in attendance, along with practically the whole of London society. 'All the world, great and small, are gone to Westminster Hall,' wrote a Mrs Delany, referring to the worries about getting tickets, 'the distress of rising early to be in time enough for a place, the anxiety about hairdressers (poor souls hurried out of their lives), mortifications that feathers and flying lappets should be laid aside for that day as they would obstruct the view from those who sit behind,' and much more. Another contemporary spoke of the trial as a sight which for 'beauty and magnificence' rivalled a coronation.

Against the resplendent setting, with the peers in crimson velvet and white ermine, the Duchess appeared a sober figure. Led in by Black Rod, she was dressed in deep mourning, hooded in black, with black gauze, black ruffles, black crape and black gloves: the perfect image of a grieving widow — except that nobody quite believed it. At different points she pretended to scribble and pretended to be taken ill 'but performed it badly'. When her own turn came to give evidence she spoke for three-quarters of an hour — all to no avail. The evidence of her secret wedding was too strong: one of the two female witnesses turned up to testify about it. And when the trial closed on 22 April, the peers were almost unanimous in their verdict.

One after another they found against her, declaring, 'Guilty, upon my honour.' The only exception was the Duke of Newcastle, who found, 'Guilty erroneously, but not intentionally, upon my honour.' No penalty was imposed, out of deference to Elizabeth's nobility (a commoner would have been burned on the hand), but she was warned that if she offended again, she risked capital punishment.

She had entered the Hall as Duchess of Kingston; she left as the Countess of Bristol. But if her opponent, Meadows, thought he could now sue for the Kingston estate, he had reckoned without the cunning of the middle-aged adventuress.

On the night after the trial ended, she organized a great party for her friends. But she did not turn up herself; instead, having got her cousin to ride around London posing in her carriage, she quietly slipped away from the capital, attained Dover and escaped by packet to Calais. Thereafter she toured the courts of Europe — still calling herself Duchess of Kingston — and lived to enjoy a scandalous old age abroad. She died in 1788 of a burst blood vessel.

The baccarat case

SIR WILLIAM GORDON-CUMMING

Cheating at cards! The accusation exploded like dynamite in the drawing rooms of Victorian high society. There had been a house party; the Prince of Wales was present; and Sir William Gordon-Cumming had been caught *cheating at cards*!

The unbelievable had occurred in September 1890, at Tranby Croft, the Yorkshire home of Mr Arthur Wilson. The shipping magnate had there entertained a dazzling assembly of guests. In addition to His Royal Highness, the future Edward VII, the party included, for example, the Earl of Coventry, Lord Edward Somerset and General Sir Owen Williams. Then there was Sir William Gordon-Cumming himself: fourth baronet, laird of some 40,000 Scottish acres, and a lieutenant-colonel in the Scots Guards. He had fought the Zulu and the Arab with honour — and now his reputation was at stake in an affair that rocked the fashionable world.

The party had assembled to attend the Doncaster Races. After dinner on the night of 8 September, the guests adjourned to play baccarat — a passion of the Prince, but not quite respectable in old-fashioned circles. In fact, the host himself disapproved of the game and did not take part. However, his son Stanley Wilson was present and saw Sir William apparently increasing his stakes in a surreptitious manner — after the cards had fallen. Horrified, young Wilson whispered news of what he had seen to Berkeley Levett, a subaltern in Sir William's regiment. 'My God, Berkeley, this is too hot,' the youth declared, and the subaltern saw the same thing. What should they do?

The two young men made no immediate accusation. Instead, Wilson told his mother, while Levett told his wife and brother-in-law, Mr and Mrs Lycett Green. And between them the little group decided to keep their counsel — for the time being.

On the next day, 9 September, the guests all went to the races together and after dinner adjourned again for baccarat. This time a white line was chalked on the green baize over which stakes were shunted. And the three new witnesses confirmed what young Wilson and Levett had suspected. Yes, the cad *was* cheating. In total, Gordon-Cumming had won £228, mostly from the Prince of Wales, who was supposed to be his personal friend!

The following day, other distinguished guests were informed: Lord Coventry, General Williams, and the Prince himself. Everyone agreed that the facts should be kept quiet to avoid a scandal. However, as a condition of keeping silence, Sir William should be made to sign an undertaking never to play cards again for the rest of his life.

Sir William was outraged when approached, and denied the charge of cheating emphatically. Nevertheless, when brought before the Prince of Wales, he was told that it was useless to deny what so many unprejudiced witnesses had alleged. And whatever his true feelings about the matter, Sir William signed the following:

> In consideration of the promise made by the gentlemen whose names are subscribed to preserve silence with reference to an accusation which has been made with regard to my conduct at Baccarat on the nights of Monday and Tuesday the 8th and 9th September, 1890 at Tranby Croft I will on my part solemnly undertake never to play cards again as long as I live.
>
> signed WILLIAM GORDON-CUMMING

Gordon-Cumming left the house the next day. But if the purpose of the document was to hush things up it proved to be remarkably ineffective. Whispers about the extraordinary contract were soon heard in society, and in no time the scandal was public knowledge. If Sir William was to keep his name in society, he had to make some sort of move. In the event, he filed an action for slander against the five people who claimed to have witnessed his cheating: young Stanley Wilson, Mrs Wilson, Berkeley Levett and Mr and Mrs Lycett Green.

The affair was a sensation. Quite apart from the amazing allegation of cheating, the Baccarat Case broke the code of silence that bound the Victorian upper classes, and brought their pleasure-loving lifestyle into the public eye. The Prince of Wales had been gambling at cards — in a house where the owner disapproved. It even transpired that the Prince had come equipped with his own baccarat counters! It seemed that the ageing Queen Victoria was at last losing her grip on the straight laces of public morals: the Naughty Nineties had arrived.

The trial opened in June 1891, and Sir William was represented by Sir Edward Clarke (who later defended Oscar Wilde in the other courtroom scandal of the decade). He made out a very plausible case for his client by claiming that Gordon-Cumming customarily played baccarat according to a betting system known as Le Coup de Trois. Since it did involve adding to stake money and winnings, it might be mistaken for sleight of hand. The initial suspicion, he pointed out, was raised by two young men aged 21 and 27 who had little experience of card-playing. The other three witnesses had merely been persuaded on the second night to think the worst of Sir William. Was there not something distasteful about this plotting against a house guest? If cheating was suspected, why was it not spoken openly? Why this underhand springing of a trap?

Sir Edward spoke forcefully. But there was a problematic issue: if Sir William was *not* cheating, why on earth had he permitted himself to sign the document? Clarke's answer was that, on the advice of Lord Coventry and General Williams, he had signed to prevent a scandal involving the Prince of Wales. The wording was, after all, very vague — it was by no means a confession of guilt.

The Prince himself had been granted a seat on the Bench and attended all of the proceedings — much to the public's astonishment. Indeed, the climax came when His Royal Highness himself was called into the box and gave his own account of events. He had been subpoenaed by Gordon-Cumming so that the world should know that the Prince never claimed to have witnessed cheating. The only 'witnesses' were the five people now charged with slander — and none of them came from the blue-blooded nobility. However, a juryman asked the Prince whether he believed the charges of cheating when he was first told about them, and the future King of England replied: 'The charges appeared to be so unanimous that it was the proper course — no other course was open to me — than to believe them.'

That was damning for Gordon-Cumming. To find in his favour would effectively mean doubting the Prince of Wales's judgement, and the jury in fact took less than a quarter of an hour to reject the charges of slander. In other words Sir William *was* a cheat, and there followed a sequence of ritual humiliations: he had to resign from the army, was expelled from his four London clubs, shunned by society and banished from every fashionable event in the calendar. The ruined baronet lived out the remaining years of his life as a social exile on one of his Scottish estates. He did not die until 1930.

Was he really guilty? His counsel, Sir Edward Clarke, always believed in his innocence, and wrote in his memoirs that the verdict was wrong. The judge, Lord Chief Justice Coleridge, has been strongly criticized for the way in which he conducted the case: he packed the court with his socialite friends, and permitted his own daughter to sit among the caricaturists who sketched the high society circus. It has even been suggested that Gordon-Cumming was framed by the Prince of Wales, because he had seduced a mistress of the future king. Whatever the truth, the Baccarat Case marked a watershed in British history: somehow, gentlemen weren't necessarily gentlemen any more.

Britain's longest trial THE TICHBORNE CLAIMANT

Inside every fat man, they say, is a thin man trying to get out. The theory would have suited Mr Arthur Orton, a Wapping-born butcher who turned the scales at 27 stone. For he hoped to prove that he was really Sir Roger Tichborne, heir to estates worth some £24,000 a year. And Sir Roger, when last seen, had been a skinny young man weighing less than nine stone!

The case was bizarre. There was absolutely no physical resemblance between Orton and the missing heir; moreover, the claimant conspicuously lacked the accent and manners of a man who had been educated at Stonyhurst and served in a Guards regiment. Orton's claim was riddled with inconsistencies, yet it baffled a nation and led to the longest trial yet in British legal history.

The affair began in April 1854, when Sir Roger Charles Doughty Tichborne sailed from Rio de Janeiro in a ship that was later lost at sea. His grief-stricken mother, the Dowager Lady Tichborne, refused to accept his death, and in 1863 began advertising worldwide for information concerning his whereabouts. In Wagga Wagga, Australia, the bankrupt emigrant Orton read the advertisements and contacted Lady Tichborne through an intermediary. He was, he wrote, her missing son. And he would like some money please.

Despite the fact that his letter was curiously misspelled, Lady Tichborne was completely taken in. Electrified by the thought that her son was still alive, she wrote begging him to come back to Europe. In

Arthur Orton

1866, Orton took up the challenge and, having raised money on the strength of his claim to be Sir Roger, he sailed for England. He arrived on Christmas Day, and on 10 January in the New Year there occurred an historic meeting in Paris, where Lady Tichborne lived. Accompanied by a solicitor, she was taken to a darkened hotel room where Orton lay, feigning illness. His face was turned to the wall; he did not utter a word. But Lady Tichborne came forward and kissed him, saying, 'He looks like his father, and his ears are his uncle's.'

Only a desperate wish to deceive herself can explain her positive identification of the fat, silent man in the curtained room. Not one other member of the family ever believed that Orton was their long-lost relative. But there were people, less closely connected with the vanished heir, who were persuaded to support his cause and testify in his favour. After all, a 12-year absence was a long time — and who but a mother could be relied on to recognize her son?

Orton boldly laid claim to the family estates which had passed to Henry Tichborne, a baby boy. The claim was resisted on behalf of the child, and Chancery proceedings began in March 1867. But it was four years before the trial opened, and in that time Orton started massing his facts about the man he had come to impersonate. In particular, he hired as servants two men who had been in Sir Roger's Guards regiment, and they supplied invaluable information. Orton memorized everything about his army days so well that 30 of the missing man's brother officers were prepared to swear that he was indeed Sir Roger Tichborne. Shortly before the trial began Lady Tichborne herself died; that was a blow to Orton's hopes. But by 11 May 1871, when the case at last came to court, he had mustered a total of over 100 witnesses prepared to testify in his favour.

Orton had done his homework; so too had his opponents. Mountains of evidence had piled up in the office of the Solicitor General — in fact, he had so much material against Orton that he seems not to have known quite where to begin. His cross-examination lasted an amazing 22 days and included much rambling, digression and obscurity. Nevertheless, devastating blows were struck against the Tichborne claimant.

For example, Sir Roger had spoken fluent French — the claimant spoke not a word. Sir Roger had received a classical education at Stonyhurst — Orton was more than a little shaky on Greek and Latin:

Solicitor General: Did you learn Virgil?

Claimant: I do not know.
Solicitor General: Did you learn Caesar? Was Caesar a Latin writer or a Greek writer?
Claimant: I cannot say, I suppose it was Greek.
Solicitor General: Is Virgil a general or statesman, or what is he?
Claimant: I told you just now, I totally forgot.
Solicitor General (producing a copy of Virgil): Look at that book. What is it, is it Latin or Greek?
Claimant: It appears to me to be Greek.

Hoots of laughter greeted this reply, and poor Orton made many similar gaffes. Additionally, he had been extremely careless during the earliest stages of his claim. For example, in her first letter to him, Lady Tichborne had signed herself H. F. Tichborne. What did the initials stand for? In Australia, Orton had made out a will in which he was required to give his mother's name, and he had guessed at 'Hannah Frances Tichborne'. He should have made inquiries: she was Henriette Félicité.

Orton's case crumbled when Lord Bellow, a Stonyhurst schoolfellow of Sir Roger, recalled that the missing man had a tattoo on his left forearm. Orton, of course, could not produce the required item for comparison. Eventually, the jury intervened and stopped the case; after 103 days Orton's claim had collapsed completely.

But proceedings did not end there. Orton was immediately arrested and brought to trial at the Old Bailey on charges of perjury and forgery. This second, criminal, trial was even longer than the first, lasting 188 days and producing as much uproar and controversy as the first. For this round, Orton produced a real show-stopper: a man named Luie who claimed to have been steward on a ship which had rescued six survivors from Sir Roger's vessel. Sensation! But not for long. Luie turned out to be a professional confidence trickster with a long police record.

In total, the whole case spanned 1,025 days. But it took the jury only 30 minutes to find Arthur Orton guilty of perjury, and he was sentenced to 14 years of hard labour. Mercifully for everyone, the prosecution had dropped the charge of forgery (of certain bonds which Orton had signed as Tichborne). Forgery was a more serious crime, and the trial would have gone on considerably longer. . . .

Lady Tichborne

Tragedy in three acts OSCAR WILDE

On 1 April 1894, the Marquess of Queensberry wrote a long and furious letter to his son Alfred Douglas. Having lambasted the youth for loafing and lolling about, the Marquess continued:

Secondly, I come to the more painful part of this letter — your intimacy with this man Wilde. It must either cease or I will disown you and stop all money supplies. I am not going to try and analyse this intimacy, and I make no charge; but to my mind to pose as a thing is as bad as to be it. With my own eyes I saw you both in the most loathsome and disgusting relationship as expressed by your manner and expression. Never in my experience have I seen such a sight as that in your horrible features. No wonder people are talking as they are. Also I now hear on good authority, but this may be false, that his wife is petitioning to divorce him for sodomy and other crimes. Is this true, or do you not know of it? If I thought the actual thing was true, and it became public property, I should be quite justified in shooting him at sight.

Alfred Douglas's reply was brief; he sent a telegram reading, 'What a funny little man you are.'

You do not have to be a particularly shrewd student of family matters to guess how that reply must have riled. And when the Marquess of Queensberry got riled, things started to happen. For in truth he was rather more than a 'funny little man'; to judge by his behaviour in the Wilde affair, the Marquess was faintly mad.

John Sholto Douglas, eighth Marquess of Queensberry, was a passionate sportsman whose name is still remembered through the Queensberry Rules, boxing's code of fair play. He had himself been an amateur lightweight champion, as well as a steeplechaser and Master of Hounds. And he was by no means afraid of controversy; an outspoken atheist, he won some notoriety by refusing to take the oath in the House of Lords, dismissing it as 'Christian tomfoolery'. His excitable temper once led him to chase after the prime minister, Lord Rosebery, with a dog whip. That same temper caused his children to detest him, and his wife to divorce him on grounds of cruelty.

Alfred Douglas, known to his mother as 'Bosie', was the Marquess's third son and a poet renowned for his flower-like good looks. It was in 1891, as a youth of 20, that he first met Oscar Wilde; and from that time an intimate friendship developed between them. Wilde was 38 and already famed as a 'decadent' and a 'poseur'. As an undergraduate at Oxford he helped to found the cult of aestheticisim, or pursuit of beauty, which was parodied in Gilbert and Sullivan's comic opera *Patience*. Wilde was the original 'greenery yallery, Grosvenor Gallery' young man, but his effete manner concealed a sharp wit which still shines through such comedies as *Lady Windermere's Fan* and *The Importance of Being Earnest*. Wilde's best work — his sparkling stage comedies — were all, in fact, written during the period in which he knew Alfred Douglas.

What did their friendship consist of? The pair were clearly infatuated with one another, and Lord Alfred was to admit, much later, that occasional 'familiarities' did take place between them. He claimed, though, that sodomy in its full sense never occurred. Nevertheless, Wilde himself was, though married, a practising homosexual, and 'Bosie' was unquestionably aware of it. Moreover, the older man wrote a number of florid letters to his young companion. These fell into the hands of blackmailers (and, in the course of time, to the Marquess of Queensberry).

The Marquess practically exploded when he received Lord Alfred's now famous telegram. Something seems to have snapped in the 'funny little man'. He threatened Lord Alfred with a thrashing, adding 'If I catch you again with that man I will make a public scandal in a way you little dream of.' Queensberry then started visiting restaurants frequented by the couple, and warned the managers not to admit them. One night he arrived unannounced at Wilde's house in Chelsea and, with a prize-fighter acting as minder, opened up a bitter confrontation which ended only when Wilde threatened to call the police. Then, on 14 February 1895, the Marquess turned up at the first night of *The Importance of Being Earnest*. He was bearing a monstrous bouquet of vegetables which he intended to present to the playwright. Wilde had been forewarned, and Queensberry was refused admittance to the theatre. But he prowled 'chattering' around for hours before finally dumping the bouquet at the stage door and leaving the scene.

By now, the Marquess was determined to create the public scandal which he had threatened. Only four days after the theatrical non-event he turned up at Wilde's club, the Albemarle, and left a card with the hall porter, instructing him to present it to the playwright. The card read, 'To Oscar Wilde posing as a som*domite.*'

It was this brief message (the key word ironically misspelled) which brought three trials and ruin to the life of Oscar Wilde. Perhaps spurred on by 'Bosie', Wilde decided that he had to prosecute his persecutor on grounds of criminal libel. The decision has often been described as foolish, for Wilde not only 'posed as' but was, after all, a homosexual — and had never been especially discreet about it. More foolish still was his decision not to confide the truth to his solicitor whom he assured, on his honour, that there was no truth in the allegation.

Oscar Wilde (standing) with Lord Alfred Douglas

Queensberry was formally arrested on 2 March, and the trial opened a month later. The Central Criminal Court at the Old Bailey was to stage each act in Wilde's three-part tragedy. Queensberry's defence was led by Edward Carson QC, who had been a fellow undergraduate of Wilde at Trinity College, Dublin. 'No doubt he will perform his task with all the added bitterness of an old friend,' quipped Wilde when he heard the news, and in fact the duel fought between the two former classmates is now remembered as a courtroom classic.

At first, Wilde was brilliant. During the early stages of his cross-examination, for example, he was questioned about a story with homosexual undertones called *The Priest and the Acolyte*; Carson tried to trap him: 'You are of the opinion, I believe, that there is no such thing as an immoral book?'

Wilde: Yes.

Carson: May I take it that you think *The Priest and the Acolyte* was not immoral?

Wilde: It was worse; it was badly written.

Carson tried to make great play of the letters written by Wilde to Lord Alfred, which had fallen into the hands of the blackmailers. There was one, for example, in which Wilde referred to 'those red rose leaf lips of yours' being 'made for the madness of kisses'. And another in which the playwright wrote of Lord Alfred being 'the divine thing I want' and complained of his 'curved lips saying hideous things to me'.

Carson: Is that an ordinary letter?

Wilde: Everything I write is extraordinary. I do not pose as being ordinary, great heavens!

These and other rejoinders often had the court rocking with laughter. But the mood changed as the names of a succession of young working-class men were brought up: valets, grooms and coachmen with whom Wilde had dined privately in curtained rooms, and to whom he had given gifts and money. Specific incidents were mentioned, and denied by Wilde. Then reference was made to a 16-year-old serving boy named Walter Grainger. Carson asked if Wilde had ever kissed the lad he replied with an attempt at airy nonchalance, 'Oh dear no. He was a peculiarly plain boy. He was unfortunately extremely ugly.'

Carson pounced: 'Was that the reason you did not kiss him?'

Wilde: Oh, Mr Carson, you are impertinently insolent.

Carson: Why, sir, did you mention that this boy was extremely ugly?

Wilde: For this reason. If I were asked why I did not kiss a door-mat, I should say because I do not like to kiss door-mats. I do not know why I mentioned that he was ugly, except that I was stung by the insolent question you put to me and the way you have insulted me throughout this hearing. Am I to be cross-examined because I do not like it?

Carson: Why do you mention his ugliness?

Again and again, as Wilde bristled and blustered, Carson interjected, 'Why did you mention his ugliness? Why? Why? Why did you add that?' Wilde was briefly reduced to speechless confusion before eventually conceding that 'at times one says things flippantly when one ought to speak more seriously.' But the damage was done; the whole tone of the proceedings had soured.

On the third day of the trial, Carson began his opening speech for the defence of the Marquess of Queensberry (by this time many in court must have forgotten that it was the Marquess who was technically on trial). And as Carson announced the names of the assorted young men he intended to put into the witness box, Wilde's counsel suddenly threw in the sponge. He announced that he was prepared to withdraw the prosecution; the Marquess was declared not guilty of libel, and the court cheered long and loud as Wilde's opponent was freed.

The tables had now turned dramatically. Wilde had effectively been exposed as a homosexual and homosexual acts were then, under the Criminal Law Amendment Act, punishable by up to two years of hard labour. Everybody assumed that the playwright would flee the country, for on the same day that Wilde dropped his case, Queensberry's solicitor sent all the witnesses' statements to the Director of Public Prosecutions. By 5 pm that day a warrant had been issued for Wilde's arrest.

Things had moved fast — but not so fast that Wilde was completely overtaken by events. He knew what was bound to come and could without difficulty have made his way to Dover and so to France. But instead — through courage or inertia — he chose to wait drinking hock and seltzer in the Cadogan hotel until at 6.30 the inevitable arrived in the form of Inspector Richards and a colleague from Scotland Yard.

Wilde's arrest was greeted with a terrible, gloating relish in the London press. His calamity seems to have released a lot of pent-up resentment against the successful dramatist; 'Few men', wrote Arthur Ransome, 'have been sent to perdition with a louder cry of hounds behind them.' His books were withdrawn from the shops, his two plays, running at the Haymarket and St James's, closed. The worst of it was that Wilde had long been living on credit and now the bailiffs moved into his Chelsea home and stripped him of every possession. Scorned, shunned and bankrupted, Oscar Wilde was ruined even before his trial began.

He reappeared at the Old Bailey, this time as defendant, on 26 April and was charged with a man named Taylor (who had been a procurer for him) on no fewer than 25 counts of gross indecency. Queensberry's private detectives had not been idle in seeking evidence among male prostitutes in London's underworld, and much sordid material had come to light. A youth named Charles Parker, for example, testified in the box that Wilde had invited him to his rooms at the Savoy and there committed acts of sodomy upon him. Later Wilde visited him at his own room: 'I was asked by Wilde to imagine that I was a woman and that he was my lover. I had to keep up this illusion. I used to sit on his knees and he used to . . . as a man might amuse himself with a girl.' (Wilde's pleasures seem to have consisted chiefly in mutual masturbation culminating in fellatio, rather than sodomy as the term is generally understood.)

In this, the second trial, Wilde was very careful not to try and show off as he had done before. Instead, looking pale and haggard, he quietly but firmly denied the charges laid against him; the case presented by his counsel was that the whole affair had been got up by, and relied on the testimony of, blackmailers. Only on one occasion did he break his reserve, and that was when he was questioned about a line in one of Lord Alfred's poems: '*I am the love that dare not speak its name.*' Was that not a clear reference to unnatural, homosexual love? Wilde replied with a moving, impromptu speech defending the spiritual love which may exist between an older and a younger man, 'when the elder man has intellect and the younger man has all the joy, hope and glamour of life before him'. He spoke of David and Jonathan, of the love pervading the works of Shakespeare, Plato and Michelangelo. When he had finished there was loud applause in court, and, almost certainly, the power of that speech helped to save Wilde at the second trial, for when the jury retired it found that it could not agree on a verdict. Accordingly the jury was discharged and, in due course, Wilde was released on bail.

The playwright enjoyed only a temporary and miserable freedom. As he sought a hotel on the first night he found himself followed by a gang of thugs, hired by Queensberry, to make sure that no manager admitted him. He ended up at the house of his alcoholic brother Willie, staggering across the threshold with the words, 'Give me shelter, Willie. Let me lie on the floor or I shall die in the streets.' (Willie Wilde only imperfectly understood the issues at stake in the trial; 'Oscar was not a man of bad character,' he once told Bernard Shaw, 'You could have trusted him with a woman anywhere.')

Friends later helped the writer out with money and accommodation, advising him to jump bail and go abroad. But Wilde flatly refused and so, when a new trial was ordered for 20 May, he returned for a third time to the Old Bailey. On this occasion, much of the earlier evidence was recapitulated, Wilde was a broken man — and the fresh jury found him guilty.

The judge, in passing sentence, was particularly severe. 'It is the worst case I have ever tried,' he thundered, and called Wilde 'the centre of a circle of extensive corruption of the most hideous kind among young men'. Passing the maximum sentence of two years' hard labour, he referred to it as 'totally inadequate in a case like this.'

Wilde swayed in the dock, his face a mask of horror. 'And I? May I say nothing, my lord?' he stammered, but the judge waved aside his protests. A few cries of 'Shame' had been heard when the sentence was pronounced in court, but in the streets outside the Old Bailey the crowd cheered and some prostitutes raised their skirts in mockery.

Wilde served his sentence at Wandsworth and later Reading, where he composed his dark *Ballad of Reading Gaol*. Afterwards, there could be no question of his continuing as a man of letters in England and he went abroad, never to return. For what was left of his life, Wilde remained an exile and a bankrupt, abandoned by all but his most loyal friends. His life had been broken by his ordeals, yet he never expressed shame either for his homosexual pleasures, or the underworld company he had kept in London. What did distress him was a sense that he had failed, somehow, in daring and panache. 'What is loathsome to me', he wrote, 'is the memory of interminable visits paid by me to the solicitor Humphreys, when in the ghastly glare of a bleak room I would sit with a serious face telling serious lies to a bald man till I really groaned and yawned. . . .'

Oscar Wilde died in a Paris hotel on 30 November 1900. Ironically, the Marquess of Queensberry died in the same year — victim of a mania by which he believed himself to be persecuted by the friends of Oscar Wilde.

After Profumo

STEPHEN WARD

There were peers and prostitutes, West Indian dope-smokers, a War Minister, a Russian Naval Attaché, a slum landlord, a mysterious Miss X, Douglas Fairbanks, two-way mirrors, whipping sessions . . . among sex scandals, the Profumo Affair was grand opera. And orchestrating the whole extravaganza, or so it seemed, was one enigmatic man named Stephen Ward.

Aged 50 at the time of his trial, Dr Stephen Ward was a successful society osteopath as well as being a talented artist. Lord Astor, a long-term friend and patient, had leased him at nominal rent a cottage on his Cliveden estate. In the summer of 1961, Conservative War Minister John Profumo was invited by the Astors to Cliveden for a house party, and as it happened, Stephen Ward had guests at his cottage too. One of them was a fun-loving Russian Naval Attaché named Captain Ivanov; another was Christine Keeler.

After dinner at the swimming pool, Profumo and Christine Keeler chanced to meet. Not much later they embarked on an affair.

It did not last long, but the reverberations were immense. For the slender-limbed and sexually voracious Keeler had a number of low-life lovers. Two of these were West Indians, John Edgecombe and Aloysius 'Lucky' Gordon, who had quarrelled violently over her. And one day when she was round at Ward's flat in Wimpole Mews visiting her friend Mandy Rice-Davies (who was staying there) Edgecombe turned up in a mini cab. He demanded to see Christine, and when refused admittance he drew a gun and fired shots at the door.

The shooting itself caused only a mild stir — until Keeler disclosed details of her promiscuous lifestyle. She said she had slept with Profumo, and also claimed to have slept with Ivanov: there was an implied threat to national security. Christine sold her story to the *Sunday Pictorial*, which, however, was persuaded that it was too hot to handle and dropped it. But rumours of the scandal spread to Parliament, where questions were asked of the Home Secretary. On 22 March 1963, John Profumo made a personal statement to the House of Commons, denying that there had ever been any impropriety between him and Keeler.

It was untrue, of course. The press would not let the story go, and more questions were asked in the House. On 4 June, Profumo came clean with a statement acknowledging that he had lied to the House, and he tendered his resignation.

Amid a scandal which rocked Macmillan's government, intense interest had focused on Stephen Ward, a man who seemed to span two different worlds: the glittering society of peers, diplomats and ministers; and a lurid subculture where nightclub girls like Christine Keeler and Mandy Rice-Davies consorted with hoodlums and racketeers. Mandy, it transpired, had for two years been the mistress of notorious slum landlord Peter Rachman. Christine through her West Indian friends frequented clubs where marijuana was smoked. Both had lived at one time or another on premises owned by Ward: what precisely was their relationship?

From April, prompted by the Home Office, the police had been investigating Ward. In June he appeared in Marylebone magistrates court on assorted charges related to prostitution, and the evidence heard there provided a sensational appetizer for his trial at the Old Bailey.

People queued overnight for places in the public gallery, camping out with blankets and Thermos flasks. The trial opened on 22 July 1963, and the waiting crowd buzzed with expectation of glimpsing the likes of Keeler, Rice-Davies and Ward himself. Already they were near-legendary figures, magical with scandal.

Ward appeared soberly dressed in the dock, a very youthful 50-year-old with a hint of the ruined Peter Pan about him. Five charges were read out relating to living on the earnings of prostitution and to procuring. To each he firmly replied, 'Not guilty,' and the trial was under way.

The prosecution opened with an account of how Keeler and Rice-Davies — both described as 'prostitutes' — had come into Ward's life.

Stephen Ward (centre) pictured leaving court

He had first met Christine at Murray's Club in 1958, and invited her down to the Cliveden cottage. At the same club he met Mandy the following year, and she also stayed at the cottage. In 1960, Ward helped to set the pair of them up in a flat in Comeragh Road, where, it was alleged, he had brought 'on a number of occasions his men friends to see them'. No specific charges were made regarding this period, though. The first count concerned living off Keeler's immoral earnings while she was staying at his Wimpole Mews flat between 1961 and 1962. The second count concerned living off Rice-Davies at the same flat for a four-month period in 1962.

These were to prove the most awkward allegations. Other, more colourful charges related to a flat at Bryanston Mews, which Ward had taken up early in 1963. Mandy Rice-Davies had lived in it with Rachman, and at one stage there had been a two-way mirror permitting viewers in the living room to watch the bedroom events without being seen. Ward had described the mirror to a certain Miss X, aged 18 and very respectable. She had firmly declared no interest in watching anything like that, and it was alleged that Ward replied, 'I don't want you to watch, I want you to perform.'

Also at Bryanston Mews, it was alleged, Ward had repeatedly procured men for a prostitute named Vickie Barrett — but kept all the money she had earned. This was the nastiest of the charges; people knew much about Keeler and Rice-Davies, but the name of Vickie Barrett was new. Was it true?

The first witness to enter the box was Christine Keeler herself, aged 21 and electrifying with sexuality. The prosecution had no difficulty in establishing her irregular lifestyle, but firm evidence against Ward was hard to elicit. Once, she said, he had introduced her to a mystery man named 'Charles' with whom she had had intercourse for money. The sum was £50.

Prosecutor: After intercourse and after you had received the £50, did you speak to Ward about it?

Keeler: I can't remember.

Prosecutor: What did you do with the £50?

Keeler: I repaid a loan with some of it to Dr Ward.

Dull stuff: it turned out that Ward had often lent her money, and she freely admitted that she had paid less than half of it back. Could it really be said that Ward was living on her immoral earnings? Was she not, rather, living on him?

Mandy Rice-Davies was more entertaining. Her pert wit had already been demonstrated in the magistrates court when asked if she was aware that Lord Astor had denied her statement that she had slept with him she had replied with the immortal line, 'Well he would, wouldn't he?' At the Old Bailey she cheerfully reeled off the list of her alleged lovers: Lord Astor, Peter Rachman, Douglas Fairbanks (who denied it) . . . she said that the first time she had intercourse with Lord Astor was at Ward's flat in Wimpole Mews.

Prosecutor: Was Ward at the flat on that occasion?

Rice-Davies: Once.

Prosecutor: When you had intercourse with Lord Astor?

Rice-Davies: It was quite normal for him to be in the flat. (*Gasps in court.*)

The judge: It was normal for Ward to be in the flat when you were having sexual intercourse with other men, was it?

Rice-Davies: Oh yes, it's quite normal isn't it? There's nothing wrong with it?

The judge reproached her for having 'gone on talking without reason for doing so', but whether she prattled or answered in monosyllables, Mandy Rice-Davies came little closer than Keeler to substantiating the prosecution's claims. Her one serious allegation was that Ward had encouraged her to sleep with a rich Indian doctor who paid money for receiving him at the Wimpole Street flat. The Indian doctor had given Ward £25 to use her room for sexual purposes, she alleged. She also stated that she had sometimes given Ward small sums of money —

perhaps £25 in all — over and above the £6 per week rent she was paying him.

Against this testimony was a denial issued by the Indian doctor himself. Her evidence was uncorroborated; and she admitted under cross-examination that the police had put pressure on her to testify against Ward. Lastly, the money involved seemed so trifling. Was this the best the prosecution could do?

Enter Miss X to tell her story about Ward's supposedly indecent proposal concerning the two-way mirror ('*I want you to perform*'). Tall and dark, the mystery woman explained, 'He said he intended watching people through it and joked that if there was a funny incident he could make a bit of spare money by people sitting round and watching.' But the truth, it transpired, was that Mandy Rice-Davies had broken the mirror before Ward even moved into Bryanston Mews; it had never been replaced — there was just a hole in the wall. Ward's sinister proposal had been no more than a bad joke.

Enter prostitute Ronna Ricardo. She had testified strongly against Ward in the magistrates' court, but now admitted she had lied there. She said she had been pressurized to give the evidence by the police and now admitted that the only man she had slept with at Ward's flat was her boyfriend 'Silky' Hawkins. Ward and another woman were there:

Prosecutor: In the other bedroom?

Ricardo: (no reply)

Prosecutor: In the same room?

Ricardo: (no reply)

Prosecutor: All four of you together?

Ricardo: (nods)

There had been a friendly foursome, no money had changed hands. Disgraceful — outrageous — but not illegal.

The prosecution's star witness was supposed to be the prostitute Vickie Barrett. She claimed that the first time she met Ward he had picked her up in Oxford Street and driven her in his white Jaguar to the flat in Bryanston Mews, where a man was waiting naked in the bedroom. Ward had given her a contraceptive and sent her in while he made coffee. After intercourse, Ward told her that he would keep the money for her and he drove her back to Oxford Street. The same thing, she said, happened with a different man in bed the next week. On a third occasion, the client in the bed did not want intercourse but a whipping, which she had administered in underwear and high-heeled shoes. After this, she said, she visited the flat two or three times a week and with horse-whip or cane beat a number of middle-aged and elderly clients. The rate was £1 a stroke — but Ward had never paid her any of the money.

The court held its breath throughout her testimony, and it presented the accused in a very unpleasant light. But was it credible? If true, Stephen Ward was the worst kind of professional ponce. Ward himself leaped to his feet in an angry outburst during her cross-examination, and in time her story was to be exposed as highly dubious. For one thing, there were guests staying at Ward's flat during the period when she was supposed to be plying her trade there — none of them had ever seen her. The flat itself had been besieged by reporters for some of the time, for it was after the Profumo scandal had broken. The whole story was faintly ridiculous anyway: how long did all these men wait naked in the bedroom? Why not wait clothed, and undress when she arrived? And would she really have trusted Ward — a complete stranger — with her earnings for weeks without claiming the money back?

It emerged very clearly at the trial that a lot of pressure had been applied to get some sort of conviction against Ward. The police had interviewed some 140 possible witnesses against him; Keeler herself had been interviewed no fewer than 24 times. Mandy Rice-Davies, meanwhile, had been prevented from leaving the country on a footling charge relating to a hire-purchase TV. Ward himself believed that he was being made a scapegoat for the whole Profumo affair and that false allegations were being made out of malice, or hope of profit from the newspapers. The strain, he wrote to police during the investigation, was driving him to the edge of nervous breakdown. He did not deny his own dissolute lifestyle, but 'It is ridiculous to say I have received money for introducing girls to men. Of course I always had pretty girls around me and took them to parties, but if this was followed up by the men and the men gave them presents, surely there is no complaint against me, and in any case I don't see anything wrong in it.'

In the witness box he was magnetic: impeccably mannered even when describing the most disreputable episodes of his life. Briefly told, his story was that he was attracted both to Keeler and Rice-Davies and had happily arranged to pay their rent when they went to live at Comeragh Road. He did so partly out of kindness and partly because he found them attractive. Also, they were broke.

Prosecutor: There are plenty of people who are broke but do not have the good fortune to have their rent paid for them.

Ward: That is true.

Prosecutor: Was the truth that you wanted to provide your friends with pretty girls?

Ward: That is completely *un*true.

Ward knew perfectly well that the two girls were promiscuous and had a 'pretty shrewd idea' that Keeler, for example, was sleeping with men at his Wimpole Mews flat. But he claimed not to know that she was receiving money for it. He denied Christine's allegations about 'Charles', and Mandy's about the Indian doctor. Rice-Davies had lived at the Mews for six weeks, he said, paying a modest £6 per week and had run up enormous telephone and electricity bills which far exceeded her contribution.

As for Vickie Barrett, he said, he twice picked her up in the West End and took her back to his flat for intercourse at £2. (It appeared from the later testimony of her friend Frances Brown that they had gone with him as a couple; Vickie 'did the business' with Ward while Frances just looked on. The rest of her story, he said, was no more than a pack of lies.

In truth, the charges relating to Vickie Barrett, Miss X and others had been effectively destroyed. There remained, however, the awkward problems of Keeler and Rice-Davies. Each had been 16 when Ward first met them, and the prosecution made much of the fact that he had been in his late forties. They admitted that they had slept with men for money, and alleged that they had passed some of their earnings on to Ward. So he was living on their immoral earnings, was he not?

The defence replied by querying whether Keeler and Rice-Davies were prostitutes in the conventional sense. Certainly they were 'good-time girls' who had received gifts and money from men with whom they had had intercourse. But they had usually had some sort of human relationship with the men who shared their beds, a relationship independent of sex. They did not pick up men indiscriminately; and

Left: Christine Keeler,
below: Mandy Rice-Davies

Keeler, at least, slept with men much more often for fun than in expectation of money.

But even supposing they *were* prostitutes, in what way could Ward be described as living wholly or in part on their immoral earnings? If he received money from them it was only in the form of rent, or the return of loans. The sums involved were trifles by comparison with his income. It was revealed at the trial that he earned some £4,000 from his practice as an osteopath and a further £1,500 as an artist—big money in 1963.

'Was this life of Ward's led for fun or profit?' asked the defence counsel in summing up.

'That is the key to the case. Was he conducting a business, living as a parasite, on the earnings of prostitution? It is a very, very wide gap and a big step between a man with an artistic temperament and obviously with high sexual proclivities leading a dissolute life, and saying he has committed the offence here of living on the earnings of prostitution.'

In retrospect, there was no real case for Ward to answer. The press today would bill him as a 'Swinging Bachelor' or 'Playboy Doc', and even in 1963, the hypocrisy of the whole trial was much commented on abroad. Nevertheless, when the judge embarked on his summing up, no-one knew quite what the verdict would be. And certainly no-one except Ward himself could have anticipated the sensational conclusion which made even the verdict seem meaningless.

On the evening of 30 July, halfway through the judge's summing up, the court adjourned at 4.30 as usual. Overnight, having given no indication of his intention beforehand, Stephen Ward took an overdose of sleeping pills. He was rushed to hospital in a serious condition.

With the whole court numbed by this amazing development, the judge decided that the trial should continue, and he completed his summing up with two policemen still sitting in attendance over an empty dock. At just after 7 pm, having deliberated for over four hours, the jury brought in their verdict. Stephen Ward was found guilty on counts 1 and 2 (relating to Keeler and Rice-Davies); not guilty on the other three counts.

Three days later, abandoned by his influential friends, Dr Stephen Ward died in hospital without regaining consciousness. In a suicide letter, he wrote of the 'horror day after day at the court and in the streets. It's not only fear — it's a wish not to let them get me. I'd rather get myself.'

Later that week, journalist Harold 'Kim' Philby, missing from Beirut since January, turned up seeking asylum in Moscow. The press had a whole new scandal to explore and the Profumo affair at last started to fade from the front pages.

CHAPTER 6

Shadows
of War

The Nuremberg Trials   **William Joyce**
Adolf Eichmann   **Pieter Menten**

Nazism in the dock

THE NUREMBERG TRIALS

Early on the morning of 14 June 1945, Joachim von Ribbentrop, former Nazi Foreign Minister, was arrested by the British on the fifth floor of his Hamburg apartment house. An acquaintance from his early life as a champagne salesman had given him away; Ribbentrop was discovered in bed, wearing pink and white pyjamas beneath which was taped a small tin of poison. When escorted from the building he brought with him a letter asking for an interview with 'Mr Vincent Churchill'. He had served as Foreign Minister for seven years — as ambassador to London for two years before that — yet he still managed to muff Churchill's name.

That was one of the most striking things about the Nazi leaders rounded up after the war: they seemed such shoddy characters; amateurish and out of scale with the nightmare they had created. In pursuing their ambitions for the Master Race, the Nazis had laid waste to nations, brought deaths measured by the million and despair on an incalculable scale. Yet, when Hitler's henchmen trooped into the Nuremberg dock they seemed such extraordinary nonentities: balding, elderly men who fussed with their headphones, looking worried, or grumpy, or bored.

What was to be done with them? During the war itself, Allied leaders had discussed precisely that question and concluded that the raw vengeance of the firing squad should be rejected in favour of formal judicial retribution. In the summer of 1945, an International Military Tribunal was formed in London and became the body responsible for trying such Nazi leaders as could be found.

Some big fish, of course, had escaped the Allies' nets.

Adolf Hitler himself had committed suicide in his bunker at the Reich Chancellery in Berlin. Dr Josef Goebbels, his chief propaganist, had followed the next day, ordering an SS assistant to shoot both him and his wife after he had poisoned his six children. Heinrich Himmler, loathsome head of the SS, had tried to save his skin by fleeing to Bavaria in disguise (he had shaved off his moustache and wore a patch over one eye). Picked up at a British checkpoint, Himmler was held for some weeks without being recognized. Not long after declaring his identity, however, he bit on a cyanide capsule and died.

Then there were the men whose fates were uncertain: nobody knew exactly what had happened to Heinrich Müller, one-time Gestapo chief; or to Martin Bormann, Hitler's deputy, or to Adolf Eichmann, faceless technician of the Final Solution. But in the drive to 'denazify' Germany, thousands of suspects had been arrested and, in the first of 13 trials at Nuremberg, 21 major figures were brought to justice. They included Party bosses, military leaders, diplomats and administrators — the intention of the tribunal was not just to try individuals but to put the whole Nazi system in the dock.

Unquestionably, the biggest fish was Herman Göring, former Luftwaffe chief and one-time successor to Hitler. A flying ace of World War I, much decorated for his bravery, Göring had been a Nazi since 1922 and reached the pinnacle of his career during the early stage of blitzkrieg warfare. However, the Luftwaffe's failure to break Britain by bombing led to a gradual fall from grace. Göring sank into pleasure-loving indolence on his country estate, grew enormously fat and took to drugs. During the Nazi collapse Göring was, in fact, expelled from the party by Hitler, and his arrest was ordered independently by Bormann. He gave himself up to the Americans to escape the possibility of assassination by some SS zealot. Under the prison regime, however, Göring shed his drug habit as well as some five stone in weight. He was in fighting trim by the time of the trial, and his mind was razor sharp.

The same could not be said for Rudolf Hess, Hitler's one-time deputy. A scarecrow whose sunken eyes glimmered beneath beetle-brows, he was a weird and baffling figure at the trial. In May 1941, Hess had bailed out of his Messerschmitt over Scotland in an apparent attempt to negotiate peace single-handed between Britain and Nazi Germany. Now he claimed to be suffering from amnesia — but was he?

Then there was Alfred Rosenberg, the Nazi theorist, whose books even Hitler regarded as unreadably obscure. And Baldur von Schirach, former Hitler Youth Leader, who gave himself up in the Tyrol. He had gone to ground there posing as 'Richard Falk, novelist' and had been writing a detective story when he learned that other Youth Leaders were being seized. In solidarity, he surrendered, writing to his wife from prison, 'I want to speak before a court of law and take the blame on myself. Through me the young have learned to believe in Hitler. I taught them to have faith in him, now I must free them from this error. Once I have had the opportunity to say this before an international court of law, then let them hang me.'

Hans Frank, civil administrator in Poland, was picked up near Hitler's mountain retreat of Berchtesgaden and handed over his 38-volume diary. It comprised a hideous indictment of Frank himself, recording the deportations, starvations, enslavements and exterminations accomplished under his authority. Frank then attempted suicide, and at the trial succumbed to religious feelings of remorse.

The vicious and depraved Julius Streicher, anti-semitic editor of *Der Stürmer*, was arrested in the same area posing as an artist. A Jewish-American officer, Major Blitt, happened to engage him in conversation and the two talked in Yiddish for a while. Then Blitt mentioned that he looked like Julius Streicher. 'How did you recognize me?' Streicher immediately barked. (In intelligence tests conducted among the Nuremberg defendants by the psychiatrist Dr Gilbert, Streicher scored lowest of all.)

These and the other prisoners were tried on four counts: *Crimes against Peace* (initiating wars of aggression); *War Crimes* (violating the laws or customs of war); *Crimes against Humanity* (murder, enslavement and deportation of civilian populations); and *Conspiracy* (implication in a common plan to commit the other three).

The trial opened on 20 November 1945, at the Palace of Justice in Nuremberg, where the vast Nazi party rallies had been held. It was to last for 218 days, involving lorry loads of documents and a cost of more than 4 million dollars. It was on the second day that the prisoners were called to answer the charges, and all pleaded not guilty, though there was some confusion in the case of Hess:

The President: Rudolf Hess.

Rudolf Hess: No.

The President: That will be entered as a plea of not guilty. (*Laughter*).

In fact one of the first major issues concerned Hess and his fitness to plead. In England he had tried several times to commit suicide, and several psychiatrists had diagnosed amnesia. In the dock he seemed frankly deranged: reading, grinning or gazing listlessly round with no apparent understanding of what was going on. Yet when asked whether he had anything to say he suddenly astonished the court by declaring in a clear, controlled voice that he had only been feigning amnesia. 'The reasons for simulating loss of memory were of a tactical nature,' he asserted, continuing that though he had some difficulty in concentrating fully, he was perfectly capable of following the trial and answering questions to defend himself. There was a moment's silence; then a burst of nervous laughter in court after which the president had to close the session. Was Hess making a true confession? Or was he now barking mad? Eventually the judges decided that his prosecution should go ahead, on the grounds that amnesia did not prevent him from presenting a defence.

Once the issue had been settled, the prosecution began to build up its case, bringing forth documents, diaries, ciné film, photographs and eyewitness accounts.

It was at Nuremberg that, for the first time, much of what is now textbook history of the Nazi period was revealed. Many secrets came to light; for example, a German intelligence officer named Lahousen described how Hitler had engineered a pretext for the invasion of Poland which started the war. Condemned German criminals had been dressed up in Polish uniforms and sent to their deaths in a fake attack on a German radio station. Their bodies were then paraded before the world's press as 'proof' of Polish 'aggression'.

It was at Nuremberg too that the first full public exposure was given to the scale of Nazi atrocities. In December, the prosecution showed a film of what the Allies had found when they opened up the concentration and extermination camps: the horrific assemblages of skeletons living and dead; the charred bits of humanity that lay heaped outside the crematoria; the pale, awkward shapes in the death pits. In the dock, very few of the defendants managed to keep their eyes trained on the screen. Afterwards, visited by the psychiatrist Dr Gilbert, they spoke of their feelings. Most denied any knowledge that such things had happened. 'Horrible, horrible,' wept Walther Funk, Nazi economist. 'No power in heaven or earth will erase this shame from my country,' sobbed Hans Fritzsche, one-time assistant to Dr Goebbels.

But more was to come in due course: the testimony of survivors who had endured torture, slave labour and experimentation. Beyond a certain point the words and images became almost numbing. From Maidenek came film of naked female prisoners lying down in pits to be shot by SS guards who grinned to camera. From Buchenwald came skins flayed from inmates' bodies and used for lampshades by the camp commandant and his wife.

And did the defendants really know nothing of these atrocities? 'Of course not,' snapped Göring. 'The higher you stand the less you see of what is going on below.' And that was the essence of the Nazis' defence, not only at Nuremberg but in the many trials which followed. At the higher levels, where decisions were made, no-one saw what was going on. At the lower levels, among the torturers and executioners, people were 'only obeying orders'. So nobody was responsible . . . not even Hitler, whose memory most of the defendants tried to shield from blame. If a scapegoat had to be found, then all were agreed that Himmler was the best candidate. 'Himmler had his chosen psychopaths to carry out these things and it was kept secret from the rest of us,' said Göring, adding that he was not a true German. Streicher agreed: 'He had a peculiar face. . . . He had Negro blood — I could tell by his head shape and hair.'

It was Göring who laid down the main lines of defence for the prisoners, and Göring who, by sheer force of personality, kept up their collective morale. The Allied cartoonists had always represented him as a fat buffoon, but he fought his case with a sharp wit and powerful intelligence that allowed him to score repeatedly against the chief American prosecutor, Mr Justice Jackson. Jackson in fact became so frustrated at one point that he tore off his earphones, 'This witness is not being responsive,' he fumed. 'It is perfectly futile to spend our time if we cannot have responsive answers to our questions. . . .' As he lapsed into incoherence, an adjournment was called.

Nevertheless, despite Jackson's unhappy performance, the fraudulence of Göring's position could not be concealed. It was he who, in the pre-war period, had created both the Gestapo and the concentration camp system. He was deeply implicated in the persecution of Jews, too. For example, one night in November 1938 the Nazis had orchestrated a mass campaign of rioting against Jews in which many people were killed. It was called the *Kristallnacht* — Night of Glass — because of the number of windows which had been smashed. It was Göring who published the decree by which all damage done was to be paid for by the Jews themselves; and by which a collective fine of one billion marks was to be raised from the Jews as atonement for the murder of a counsellor of the German Embassy in Paris.

Göring had personally looted some £20 million of art treasures from occupied Europe. He was implicated in the murder of escaped officers after the celebrated break-out at Stalag Luft III. And though he claimed to know nothing of the extermination programme he had signed decrees relating to it. Who if not Göring was guilty?

None of his co-defendants could match him for stature in the witness box. Hess refused to testify; Ribbentrop rambled pathetically; Streicher practically foamed at the mouth. And Dr Ernst Kaltenbrunner, former head of the Reich Main Security Office, was reduced to blatant lying to try and save his neck. His position had made him a key figure in the Final Solution; yet, twitching in the dock, he denied everything — even having heard of the extermination programme. This despite sworn affadavits that described how he had ordered the destruction of the Warsaw Ghetto, relished demonstrations of

Defendants at the Nuremberg trials

execution, and laughed in a gas chamber at Mauthausen. Curiously, Kaltenbrunner called as his chief witness Rudolf Hoess, Commandant of the death camp at Auschwitz (1940–43). Some of the most chilling evidence in the trial was given by this specialist exterminator, who spoke with professional pride of the 2,500,000 people he had liquidated (and with regret of the further half-million who had died 'accidentally' from starvation and disease). When Kaltenbrunner returned from the witness box, almost all his co-defendants shunned him.

It was easy to see why a man like Kaltenbrunner had to be brought to justice. But there were more problematic cases. In the dock at Nuremberg sat the soldiers Wilhelm Keitel and Alfred Jodl; the sailors Dönitz and Raeder. Granted that all war is ugly, had they really behaved more criminally than their Allied counterparts? Than the man responsible, for example, for dropping atomic bombs on Hiroshima and Nagasaki? 'The victor will always be the judge, the vanquished the accused,' Göring observed cynically at the trial. And there were some obvious inconsistencies in the way that justice was applied. For example, members of the German high command were arraigned for initiating wars of aggression; yet nobody arraigned Russian generals for attacking Finland in 1939; or conspiring to permit the invasion of Poland under the Nazi-Soviet Pact.

There were other controversial cases, notably that of Hjalmar Schacht. He was a brilliant financier who had done much to raise funds for the Nazis during the early period of their rise to power. He had been president of the Reichsbank and Minister of Economics under Hitler, and since the Allies wanted to put the whole Nazi hierarchy in the dock, he seemed the obvious man to represent high finance. But Schacht argued his case powerfully at the trial: he had never been a member of the Nazi party, he had opposed Nazi policies and complained personally to Hitler about the persecution of the Jews. His only motive in helping the Nazis had been to save Germany from financial ruin. In 1939, when it became clear that Hitler's ambitions were leading to war, Schacht had resigned from the Reichsbank. He claimed to have conspired against Hitler, and certainly was arrested after the July Bomb Plot of 1944, and sent to a series of concentration camps. In fact, Schacht was taken from captivity in Dachau to face trial at Nuremberg — a weird irony. He claimed not to understand what he was doing in the dock with 'these criminals'.

Judgement for all the defendants was reached on 30 September 1946, and sentence was passed the following day. Schacht, in fact, was one of the three men acquitted and freed by the court (the others were the diplomat Papen and the propagandist Fritzsche). Admiral Dönitz received 10 years; Neurath, diplomat and administrator, received 15; Albert Speer, architect and a key figure in war production, and Schirach received 20 years each. Hess was sentenced to life imprisonment, as was the economist Funk and Grand Admiral Erich Raeder. The other men in the dock were all sentenced to death by hanging, along with Martin Bormann, who was tried and sentenced in his absence.

The hangings were scheduled to take place in the prison gymnasium on 16 October. However, on the evening beforehand, Hermann Göring managed to cheat the hangman by taking a phial of cyanide which he had mysteriously managed to conceal about his cell or person despite searches by the guards. He was found, blue-faced and frothing from the lips, and was dead before a doctor arrived.

The next day the other hangings went ahead as planned on a black-painted gallows in the gymnasium. The bodies, including that of Göring, were driven away for cremation — nobody knows quite where. However, some have suggested that they may have been cremated in the ovens at Dachau, the former concentration camp, not far from Nuremberg itself.

Should Lord Haw-Haw have hung

WILLIAM JOYCE

'Jairmany calling . . . This is Jairmany calling. . . .' The plummy vowels were first heard on the airwaves on 18 September 1939, only a fortnight after Britain declared war on Germany. And the broadcaster continued to address the British public — from Zeesen, Hamburg, Bremen and elsewhere — throughout the war, right up until 30 April 1945. The voice harped on incessantly about the good life enjoyed in Germany, the invincibility of the Führer's armies, and the forthcoming Allied humiliations. Sometimes there seemed to be an uncanny accuracy in the forecasts made by the voice, and the British authorities grew concerned about effects on civilian morale.

But something in those hoity-toity tones rang false; something hinted more at the 'toff' of music-hall comedy than at the authentic voice of an English gentleman. A journalist at the *Daily Express* perfectly captured the ludicrous undertones when he nicknamed the broadcaster Lord Haw-Haw.

The name stuck. Suddenly, the sinister component of the propaganda seemed to evaporate and the speaker became a figure of fun. *Lord Haw-Haw the Humbug of Hamburg* was just one of the comic songs sung about him, and if people still tuned in to him deliberately they did so, as often as not, for a laugh.

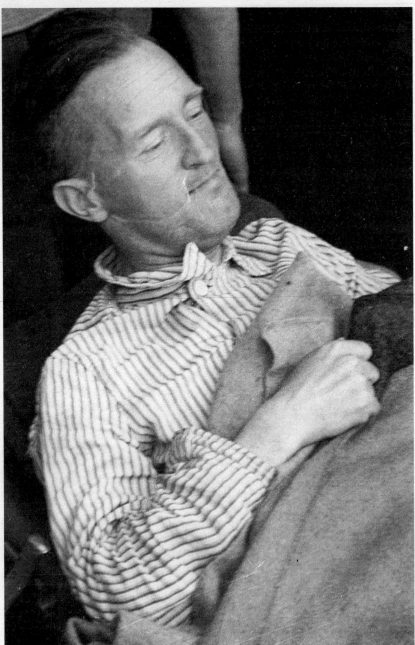

Lord Haw-Haw alias William Joyce

Nevertheless, the Germans did not finance his broadcasts for fun. When the war was over, it was not surprising that charges should be brought against him if he were, as it seemed, a British traitor. But who was Lord Haw-Haw? Was he really British at all?

It transpired that the man behind the voice was one William Joyce, born in Brooklyn, New York, in April 1906. This was clearly established at his trial, where it was also learnt that his family moved to Ireland three years later. For Joyce's father, it was a homecoming; he had emigrated from Ireland many years before. But he had taken up American nationality before his son was born, so that there was never any serious question on this important issue: William Joyce was an American, both by birth and by paternity.

At the age of 15, Joyce came to England to pursue a long course of studies. And in 1933, he took a step of immense future significance. On 4 July he applied for a British passport, falsely claiming that he was born at Galway in Ireland, and so a British subject by birth. The passport was duly issued, and Joyce was to renew it in due course.

Meanwhile he developed a strong connection with the extreme Right in British politics. Joyce was an early member of the British Fascists, and acquired a slash in the face from a razor while street fighting with Communists. From 1933–37 he was a member of Sir Oswald Mosley's British Union of Fascists, during which period charges of assault and riotous assembly were lodged against him (Mosley himself once referred to Joyce as 'an offensive little beast'). In 1934, he also formed his own group, the National Socialist League, which survived until 1939. Then, on the eve of war, Joyce dissolved the group and went to Germany. He was there when war broke out, and remained there to deliver his notorious broadcasts.

In May 1945, Joyce was picked up near the Danish border by two British officers, and was shot in the leg during the arrest. Brought to England the following month, he was arraigned on a charge of high treason.

His trial opened at the Central Criminal Court in September 1945 and, from the outset, the important issue concerned Joyce's precise status as a citizen. You might think it was fairly simple: if Joyce was British then a treason charge made sense; if he was an alien, how could he be a traitor? In fact, the case was much more complex than that, involving major principles of law.

The judge, Mr Justice Tucker, ruled it beyond doubt that Joyce's true nationality was American. There was no way in which he could be called British (in September 1940, Joyce was granted German nationality, which made British claims doubly hard to assert). But from 18 September 1939, when he started broadcasting, to 2 July 1940, when his British passport expired, Joyce was a British passport holder. It did not matter whether the passport was applied for fraudulently or not; Joyce owed allegiance to the British Crown and it was only up to the jury to decide whether during that limited period he had 'adhered to the King's enemies' abroad.

Once the issue was settled, there was little contest over the facts. Obviously, Joyce *had* adhered to the King's enemies abroad, and on 19 September 1945 he was convicted and sentenced to death.

An appeal failed. Then the Attorney General permitted a rare second appeal on the grounds that it involved a 'point of law of exceptional public importance'. The case was heard in the House of Lords, which upheld the earlier trial verdict, so establishing a new and controversial precedent. Essentially, it was decided that in holding a British passport, Joyce had every right to expect the protection of the British Crown. Being protected by the Crown, Joyce automatically owed it allegiance.

There were many who questioned the ruling. Realistically, what protection did Joyce expect from the British crown in Nazi Germany? He was an alien; the broadcasts were made on foreign soil; the crown, it was said, had no jurisdiction whatever. And there was another, more general, feeling that whatever the technicalities, the penalty exceeded the crimes. Lord Haw-Haw did not belong in the same category of culprits as, for example, the exterminators of Auschwitz and Treblinka.

It made no difference; there was no reprieve. The voice that had called from Jairmany was silenced forever on 3 January 1946, when William Joyce was hanged at Wandsworth.

The Jerusalem judgement ADOLF EICHMANN

When top Nazis were interrogated after the Third Reich's collapse, they were questioned especially about the extermination programme, in which more than six million people perished. Who was responsible for that colossal human disaster? It was Hitler, of course, who decreed that there should be a Final Solution to the Jewish problem; Himmler and Heydrich were often mentioned too. But there was another name which cropped up again and again in the transcripts of interrogations and trials. That name was SS Lieutenant Colonel Adolf Eichmann.

For some 15 years after the end of hostilities he remained a shadowy figure whose fate was unknown and who was little mentioned in the popular war histories. The nature of Eichmann's work was such that he had reason to be shy of cameras — practically no photographs had survived. Though named by the United Nations War Crimes Commission as a wanted man, Adolf Eichmann remained faceless, elusive — one of Nazism's enigmas. Then, on 23 May 1960, the Israeli prime minister David Ben-Gurion electrified the world by declaring that Eichmann had been located and brought to Israel, where he would be tried for his part in the Holocaust.

The circumstances of his escape and capture were as sensational as any thriller-writer could invent. Eichmann, it transpired, had fled from the collapsing Third Reich by means of a secret SS escape line which took him via Austria to an Italian monastery, where he was issued with forged papers in the name of 'Ricardo Klement'. Under that identity he had obtained an Argentine visa and gone to live in Buenos Aires, where, in 1952, his wife and children had joined him. Sheltered by the fellowship of exiled Nazis, he had found no difficulty in getting work; eventually he had enjoyed a decently paid position with the firm of Mercedes-Benz.

Eichmann, though, was tracked down by the Israeli Secret Service and kept for a while under clandestine observation until he could be positively identified. Then, in May 1960, he was grabbed at a bus stop on his way home from work; bundled into a car by a four-man snatch team, he was driven to a safe house, where, without offering resistance, he confessed to his identity. Additionally (perhaps fearing that the alternative was immediate death), he agreed to be conducted back to Israel for trial.

The impact of these events was immense. Throughout the world, Eichmann's abduction and forthcoming trial were headline news, and their implications were hotly debated. Did Eichmann's crimes justify this breach of international law? Could he be guaranteed a fair trial in Israel — a nation born from the ashes of the Holocaust? Should he be tried at all — was it not better now to forget the horrors of the war?

The trial itself was on trial, as was the youthful state of Israel. For these reasons, the whole affair had to be conducted with meticulous correctitude. Eichmann was given every facility, including his own defence lawyers from West Germany. The utmost care was taken to provide open press coverage: TV cameras ran throughout the whole proceedings, and some 700 foreign correspondents were accommodated along with many internationally known lawyers and historians. Within Israel itself, interest was so intense that bus drivers with transistors, listening to witnesses give evidence, were known to stop their vehicles dead in the streets at moments of high emotion.

Adolf Eichmann arrived at the crowded Jerusalem court on the morning of 11 April 1961, to a collective sharp intake of breath. Thin-lipped and bespectacled, he entered the glass-walled dock looking as respectable as any of those who craned from the public benches to try and fathom the mystery of his soul. Like the men who had packed the dock at Nuremberg, Eichmann was frankly disappointing: he looked so appallingly normal.

The trial began with a debate on the legality of the proceedings; the possible bias of the Israeli judges, the validity of Israel's Nazi Punishment law and the issue of the abduction. Each of these was explored at length before the prisoner made his pleas of not guilty to the 15-point indictment against him. At last the Attorney General, Gideon Hausner, opened for the prosecution:

'As I stand here before you, Judges of Israel, to lead the prosecution of Adolf Eichmann, I do not stand alone. With me, in this place and at this hour, stand six million accusers. But they cannot rise to their feet and point an accusing finger toward the man who sits in the glass dock and cry: "I accuse." For their ashes were piled up in the hills of Auschwitz and in the fields of Treblinka, or washed away by the rivers of Poland. . . .'

The prosecution's aim in the weeks that followed was twofold: to describe the hideous nature and scale of the crimes committed by the Nazis; and to establish Eichmann's key role in their commission. There was no difficulty on the first point: within Israel were all too many witnesses to the martyrdom of European Jewry, and only a select few were called. For example, Mrs Rivka Yoselewska, originally from Zagorodski in eastern Poland, described how one of the dreaded *Einsatzgruppen* or extermination squads had descended on the Jewish quarter of her town one day in 1941. The population was surrounded by SS men, who, with whips and shouts, herded them like animals into the town square, where they were kept overnight without food or water. Next morning, exhausted by terror and fatigue, they were marched out and commanded to undress by a huge open pit. Then they were lined up, shot one by one in the back of the head and kicked into the ditch.

Mrs Yoselewska saw her mother, grandmother, sister and six-year-old daughter murdered before her eyes. But by chance, the bullet destined for her only grazed her head and she was kicked alive into the mass grave from which she later emerged, choking and struggling, amid the suffocating weight of bodies. Not all were dead; many were still writhing, 'and were biting at me and pulling me down'. But the Germans were gone, she managed to pull free. She lingered like a ghost in the area for three days, hoping to die, before being helped by a farmer to flee into the forest, where she joined the partisans.

Rivka Yoselewska had suffered a heart attack under the strain of

Adolf Eichmann

> **The Witches of Salem**
> Perhaps the most famous witchcraft trials in history opened at Salem,
> Massachusetts, in 1692. Ten young girls accused Tituba, West Indian
> slave to a local preacher, of bewitching them. Under flogging, Tituba
> falsely accused two confederates and a flood of hysterical charges and
> counter-charges ensued.
>   A special court was set up to try the accused, but the judges
> themselves succumbed to the mood of public panic and hundreds
> of people were imprisoned: 14 women and 5 men were hanged,
> while another person was pressed to death (crushed under weights
> — a traditional punishment for those who refused to plead).
>   Before the end of the year, the mania had subsided. The court was
> dissolved; in May 1693, Governor Phelps ordered the release of all
> prisoners held on witchcraft charges, and bereaved families received
> compensation.

waiting to testify. But she spoke clearly in a quiet voice for almost an
hour and a half. There was sobbing in the audience. The defence
counsel did not cross-examine.

In fact, Eichmann's lawyers wisely refrained from questioning at
length any of the survivors of Nazi atrocity who filed into the witness
box to tell their stories. They spoke of SS sadism; of pseudo-medical
experiments; of the systematic terror by which whole masses of camp
inmates were turned into dehumanized, skeletal robots; of the ovens
and chimneys at Auschwitz, which offered the only exit from the living
hell.

What, though, of the man in the glass cubicle? What was his role in
the catastrophe?

Adolf Eichmann had joined the Nazi Party in 1932 at the age of 26.
As a member of the SD (the exclusive security service of the SS) he
quickly made a name for himself as a specialist in Jewish affairs.
Assigned to the Jewish Department, he taught himself Hebrew and
Yiddish and always prided himself on his deep knowledge of Jewish
culture. It came in useful when through a mixture of threats and guile
he was to deceive the leaders of Jewish communities into submitting
their people to Nazi designs. Attached to the Viennese Gestapo, Eichmann initiated a scheme for the mass emigration of Jews from Austria.
Cold arrogance was his chief trait: at the first opportunity he would
slap a Jewish functionary in the face — then they could get down to
business.

Throughout the war, Eichmann headed the Jewish Department at
the Gestapo. In this capacity he became responsible for all adminis-
trative matters concerning the round-up of Jews; their isolation in
ghettos; their deportation to concentration and death camps. Obvi-

ously, he was not a man who could plead like others before him that he 'did not know' about the Final Solution. Instead, he adopted the alternative line that he was 'only obeying orders'.

While awaiting trial he was questioned at great length by Israel's Chief Inspector Less. The result of their conversation amounted to 3,564 typewritten pages, which were produced as evidence in court. Eichmann presented himself as little more than a 'transport officer', a very minor official who was used to discipline from childhood and who in the SS achieved a total, 'corpse-like' obedience. He said that he knew it was 'meaningless' to offer this as a defence and that although there was no blood on his hands he was 'inwardly ready to expiate for the dark events'. He even made the weird declaration that 'Should it serve as a greater act of expiation, I would even be prepared to hang myself in public as a deterrent example for anti-Semites of all the countries on earth.' This dramatic offer was never, of course, taken up; and it contrasted strongly with his refusal to express regret in court. 'To my mind,' he told the Attorney General, 'regrets do not help nor do they change matters. They cannot bring the dead to life. Repentance is a matter for small children.'

Eichmann's claim to be a mere transmitter of orders also contrasted strongly with statements he had made before his kidnapping to a Dutch Nazi journalist named Sassen. While hiding in Argentina, Eichmann had held long taped conversations with the writer, who was compiling the Nazi version of the extermination story. It was clear from these tapes that Eichmann had thrown himself zealously into his work: 'I was *not* just a recipient of orders. Had I been that I would have been an imbecile. I was an idealist.'

For legal reasons not all of the Sassen tapes could be used in court. But it was clear as the trial progressed that Eichmann was much more than a minor bureaucrat. It was shown that he attended the notorious Wannsee conference in January 1942, at which it was first determined that some 11 million Jews should be liquidated, either through being worked to death or through 'special treatment' (execution). At Wannsee, ways and means of killing were debated. Subsequently, if anyone at the Foreign Office had any technical, organizational or material needs they were to contact Adolf Eichmann. At Nuremberg, Hermann Göring had called Eichmann 'all powerful on the question of the extermination of the Jews . . . (he) had practically unlimited power to declare who was to be killed'.

Eichmann was no cog in the machinery of annihilation — he was a dynamo. Tirelessly he scoured Europe for Jews to fill up his doomed quotas for deportation, appearing unexpectedly now in France, now in Czechoslovakia, now in Belgium, to accelerate and encourage the purge. 'The great forwarding agent of death,' was how one top Nazi, Wilhelm Hoettl, had described him. And Rudolf Hoess, Commandant at Auschwitz, had written, 'He showed himself to be completely obsessed with the idea of destroying every single Jew he could lay hands on.'

For Eichmann, there could be no exceptions to the rules of the Solution. Once, a Latvian Jewess named Jenni Cozzi was caught in a Nazi dragnet and turned out to be the widow of an Italian high officer. The man's friends pressed for her release and her cause was taken up by the Italian Embassy, the Italian Fascist Party and even the Nazi Foreign Office. But Eichmann would not yield her up.

Then there was the case of the Jewish airmen. Towards the end of the war, Hitler had ordered that all Jews among Allied airmen who bailed out over Germany should be executed. The Luftwaffe's General Karl Koller described the shooting of men in uniform as murder and pleaded on their behalf. Even the loathsome Ernst Kaltenbrunner, hanged for war crimes at Nuremberg, relented. But not Eichmann. Eichmann refused to listen.

It was, in fact, towards the end of the war that Eichmann's obsessive character became most apparent. In March 1944 the Final Solution had not yet been applied to Hungary, and Himmler ordered, 'Send down to Hungary the master in person.' The 'master', of course, was Eichmann, who was instructed to 'comb the country from East to West; send all the Jews to Auschwitz as quickly as possible'.

Eichmann obeyed and by May the mass deportations had started. Truckloads of Jews 'packed together like herrings' were dispatched to Auschwitz at rates of up to 14,000 a day. When almost half a million had made the hellish journey, there still remained some 400,000 in Budapest, the capital, itself.

Eichmann conceived the last round-up at a pace that worried both his own Foreign Office and the puppet government of Hungary. The Allies had by now landed in France; neutral governments were protesting about the fate of the Jews; even hardened veterans of Nazism were getting worried about exposure. Hitler insisted that the Budapest purge go ahead, but he was prepared to make exception in the cases of some 9,700 families whom the Hungarians themselves wanted to let emigrate to Palestine.

Incredibly, Eichmann defied Hitler's order, protesting that, 'the Jews in question are without exception important biological material, many of them veteran Zionists, whose emigration to Palestine is most undesirable'. He asked for a new decision from the Führer.

There followed a complicated battle between Eichmann and the Hungarian authorities, who stopped all deportations from Budapest. Eichmann managed to get a trainload of 15,000 Jews over the border and on its way to Auschwitz. The Hungarians protested to Berlin, but Eichmann had won a significant victory. Soon after, Hitler cancelled the exit permits for those Jews who had been offered emigration.

Meanwhile a fantastic scheme had been brewing, probably at the instigation of Himmler. A million Jewish lives would be spared if the west would supply ten thousand trucks to the SS for use on the Eastern Front. Eichmann was instructed to handle the secret negotiations in Budapest, through a Jewish intermediary named Brand. It is clear from the testimony of a subordinate that Eichmann disliked the whole project and hoped to see it frustrated. Nevertheless, he summoned Brand to a hotel meeting, where, as Brand testified, he yelled, 'You know who I am. I carried out the actions in Europe, in Poland, in Czechoslovakia; now it is Hungary's turn. . . . Blood for goods! What do you want: fertile women, working men, children, old people? Speak up.' At another meeting he said, 'A million Jews for ten thousand trucks; that is cheap, so they must be factory-new trucks, with all the proper accessories and equipment.' Later still, when Brand went abroad to try to make the required arrangements, Eichmann told Mrs Brand (who had been kept hostage): 'Cable your husband that if he does not come back at once I'll put the mills of Auschwitz into motion.'

The monstrous blackmail may always have been fraudulent — an attempt to divide Russia from her Western allies. In all events it ultimately failed, much to Eichmann's satisfaction; under cross-examination at the trial he admitted that his heart had never been in it.

In October 1944 a fully fledged Nazi government was installed in Budapest and Eichmann at last got the go-ahead for the mass deportation of Jews from the capital. The Red Army had broken through on the Eastern Front and was marching on Budapest; the railway system was wrecked and such trains as were available were urgently needed by the military. How could Eichmann proceed with the deportations? The 'master' had a suggestion: why not march the Jews out of Hungary on foot?

Nothing could more clearly illustrate his lethal zeal for his work. The Reich was crumbling all around, but still the purge must go on.

No Sex Please, You're on Trial
The mass trials of terrorists in Italy have created problems unforeseen by the judiciary. In August 1983, twins were born in prison to a woman who had conceived them in the dock with her lover.

At Turin only a month later, Sonia Benedetti, one of 135 alleged Primea Linea terrorists on trial, proudly told journalists that she too was expecting a baby — conceived in the dock with her husband.

At Milan in July 1984, a judge ordered that male and female defendants on trial on terrorist charges be separated. Two of them had been involved in 'sexually explicit' activity in his courtroom and enough, after all, was enough.

In November 1944, Jews were marched from Budapest to Austria in their thousands. An International Red Cross report read,

Wherever we went, throughout the length of the highway, we witnessed horrible scenes. The deportees marched in endless lines, ragged, starved, and exhausted, including old people who could hardly drag themselves along. The gendarmes drove them on with rifle butts, truncheons and whips. They had to cover 30 kilometres daily. . . .

The marches ended in November only when Himmler himself ordered the stoppage of the extermination programme. He clearly knew Eichmann's fanaticism, for he demanded that he come to Berlin and declare face to face that he would obey the order to stop the killing. Would he submit? In terror, Eichmann replied, 'Yes, Reichsführer.' But later, as the whole fabric of the Reich was disintegrating, Eichmann declared in a speech to his staff that 'I will jump with joy into my grave in the knowledge that I drag with me millions of Jews.'

This was one of the most damning statements reported of Eichmann, and he was closely questioned about it. In the glass dock at Jerusalem, Eichmann tried to maintain that he had only alluded to 'enemies of the Reich'. But the prosecution then sprang on him his own signed statement, made during the pre-trial investigation, where he had referred to the speech and specified 'five million Jews'. Yes, Eichmann eventually admitted, he had spoken of Jews — but the remark was being wrongly interpreted.

Found guilty on all counts, Adolf Eichmann was sentenced to death on 15 December 1961. An appeal failed, and on the night of 31 May 1962 he was taken from his cell to be hanged. 'I had to obey the rules of war and my flag,' were the last words he spoke before the trap door opened. Afterwards, his body was cremated and the ashes were deposited at sea, well beyond Israel's three-mile limit.

Boiling to Death

The great British poisoners of the last hundred years could count themselves lucky that they did not live in an earlier era. Horrible to relate, the capital punishment of boiling to death was once on the statute book for poisoning. The Act was passed under Henry VIII in 1531, and the occasion was the trial of a man named Richard Rosse (or Coke), who was alleged to have poisoned 17 people in the household of the Bishop of Rochester; two of them, a man and a woman, died. Found guilty and duly sentenced, the cook was publicly boiled at Smithfield.

Margaret Davy, a young woman, suffered the same fate for a similar crime on 28 March 1542. The Act was repealed five years later.

The collector PIETER MENTEN

On 22 May 1976, Holland's biggest-circulation newspaper, *De Tele-graaf*, published a full-page article on millionaire art collector Pieter Nicolaas Menten. The occasion was an important sale of some of his art treasures, which were to be auctioned at the Amsterdam branch of Sotheby. But the 77-year-old Menten spoke more generally about his life, the origins of the collection, and of how his family fortunes had suffered during the war.

In Israel, journalist Chaviv Kanaan read a translation of the piece with mounting disgust. For he knew a different version of the million-aire's wartime past. Pieter Menten, he believed, had operated with SS extermination units in the region of eastern Poland from which Kanaan originated. Menten was responsible for the death of practically all of Kanaan's family. And the core of his great art collection was three railroad cars packed with treasures plundered from Jewish owners, which Menten had brought back from Poland to Holland in 1943.

The sale must not go ahead. Those art works were stained with the blood of martyred families. Kanaan broke the story in Israel with a newspaper piece headlined, NAZI CRIMINAL AUCTIONS ART STOLEN FROM THE JEWS.

The story was followed up in Holland by Hans Knoop, editor of the news magazine *Accent*, who began to investigate Kanaan's charges from the European end. In the furore which followed, the auction was cancelled, Menten retreated to the seclusion of his luxury mansion near Blaricum, and was there besieged by reporters. (One photo-grapher working for the German magazine *Der Stern* was arrested for having himself hoisted by crane in a skyhook bucket over the 20-ft estate walls to obtain telephoto pictures of the millionaire.)

As more and more documentary material came to light, an order for Pieter Menten's arrest was taken out. But someone must have tipped the millionaire off, for on the eve of the arrest, Menten suddenly disappeared from his Blaricum mansion. A reward was offered by the Dutch Ministry of Justice, Interpol was informed and in December 1976 the missing millionaire was hunted down at a Swiss hotel and taken into custody. Extradited, he was taken back to the Netherlands for trial.

It was not, in fact, the first time that Menten had been hauled up before the Dutch judiciary. After the war, various charges of collabor-ation had been brought against him, including enlisting in a foreign army and stealing art objects from Jews in eastern Poland. But although a fat dossier had been compiled, no murder charges had then been brought against him and he had got off lightly with a minimal

Pieter Menten

eight-month sentence. The chief reason for his lenient treatment was that a Jewish antique dealer had testified in his favour, asserting that Menten had helped him to escape from the Nazis. This, it appeared, was true; but Menten and the dealer were bound together by mutual financial interests. Moreover, the dealer had fled to Palestine early in 1941, shortly before the alleged atrocities in eastern Poland began. The dealer was still alive when the new case opened; significantly, he refused to come to Holland and speak again on Menten's behalf.

The trial opened in May 1977, by which time the eyes of the world had turned on to the case and the charges against Menten were widely publicized. The prosecution alleged that, before the war, Menten had acquired extensive interests in lumber in the wooded region of Lemberg (now Lvov) of eastern Poland, which now lies in the Soviet Ukraine. He was well known there, to both the local Polish and the Jewish communities. In 1939, the area was overrun by the Russians and Menten lost almost all of his properties, including an estate near the village of Podhorodze.

Menten fled to the German-occupied part of the country and quickly fell in with the Nazis, to whom he offered his services. The prosecution contended that, although he never formally joined the SS, he served them in a freelance capacity as a member of the *Einsatzkommando*, or extermination squad, of Dr Eberhard Schöngarth. The *Einsatzkommandos* were formed specially to liquidate Jews and Bolsheviks in areas recaptured from the Soviets. Menten had been identified by several eyewitnesses as heading the executioners at Podhorodze and the nearby village of Urycz, where he was well known for his pre-war activities.

According to the prosecution, Menten had also gone on plundering expeditions with Schöngarth, hoarding art works confiscated from Jewish collections and keeping them in private warehouses instead of handing them over to the German authorities. Schöngarth and Menten had, it was alleged, been tried on Himmler's orders in 1942 and received short prison sentences for defrauding the Reich in this manner.

The case against Menten was amply documented. Wartime photographs of him in German uniform were submitted. Schöngarth (before being hanged for war crimes in 1946) had remembered Menten and identified him from photographs, stating that he had permitted the Dutchman to use the uniform and rank of Hauptscharführer in his unit. Documents relating to Menten's 1942 trial had also survived. But the most telling evidence concerned the massacres in eastern Poland.

Four Polish women from Podhorodze described how on 7 July 1941 Menten had arrived at the village in SS uniform accompanied by soldiers. He was carrying a pistol and clearly in command. The Jews were rounded up and shot, one by one, before being kicked into a newly dug pit. Three non-Jewish Poles succumbed to the same fate: his former estate manager Novicky, Novicky's wife and brother-in-law. All remembered how Mrs Novicky remained standing after the first shot, failing to fall into the grave. It was Menten who kicked her in

— still alive. The whole village had been forced to watch the executions and one of the women was ordered to pick a bouquet of flowers for Menten and his crew.

Michael Hauptmann, a witness who had emigrated from Poland to Sweden, arrived at the court to describe the massacre at Urycz, which took place on 27 August. He said he had watched from a hidden position as more than 200 Jews were herded together, including his parents and his four sisters. A plank was placed across the improvised grave and the Jews were made to walk across in groups of ten. At the centre, according to Hauptmann, they were told to stop and Menten gave the order to fire. When the last batch had been killed, he passed round a large brandy bottle, from which each of the executioners took a swig. Hauptmann himself was discovered afterwards and shot by a Ukrainian nationalist, who left him for dead at the edge of the pit. He recovered, however, and remembered vividly how, after heavy storms, rain soaked into the hastily covered grave so that it was soon seeping blood and mud.

The various eyewitness accounts and affadavits came from survivors on both sides of the Iron Curtain. There could be no question that the massacres were real, for shortly before the trial Soviet authorities had opened up the graves to discover the skulls and bones; odd braids of hair; children's shoes and other relics of the atrocities. Nor, tragically, were they unique. It was estimated that Schöngarth's units alone had murdered some 6,000 people in just such a manner between July and August 1941.

What defence could Menten possibly offer against such evidence? His reply was that the whole case was a KGB set-up. He had never worn a German uniform; the photographs were fakes; the incriminating documents were forgeries. Witnesses were lying or, at best, deluded in identifying him as the man present at the executions. In court Menten behaved in a peppery manner, frequently interrupting with scathing jibes and complaints. 'This isn't a real trial, it's a KGB stunt, a show trial,' he protested at one point.

More persuasively, his defence tried to exploit the inevitable discrepancies which existed in the testimonies of witnesses trying to recall events more than 30 years old. The most serious of these was that some people stated that Menten only ordered the killings at Podhorodze; others that he had participated by shooting. There was an element of doubt here — and where there was doubt there was a possibility of acquittal.

In the event, the court's finding was meticulous. The charges involving the Urycz massacre were dismissed through insufficient evidence directly incriminating Menten (though the presiding judge took the unusual step of declaring it 'very likely' that Menten did participate). As for Podhorodze, however, the evidence of participation was overwhelming. Judge Schroeder reflected that lust for material things had obviously been Menten's guiding principle; after he lost his Polish properties he had returned seeking revenge. He was sentenced to 15 years' imprisonment for killing 'with cool and calm deliberation the residents of the Polish village of Podhorodze'.

But the story did not end there. Menten appealed to the Supreme Court against the verdict; and, surprisingly, he was released on a technicality. Throughout Holland there were mass demonstrations, headed by members of the Jewish community and of the former Dutch resistance. The state of Israel requested extradition, and although this was not granted, the Supreme Court did reject the grounds on which the earlier appeal had been granted and ordered a retrial.

Menten collapsed when a new warrant was issued for his arrest, and his ill health caused the new trial to be suspended. Meanwhile, an armed gang tried to burn down a house of his in Eire (his Blaricum mansion had already been largely destroyed when a former SS man, claiming to act out of repentance, hurled a home-made bomb at it).

The retrial opened in May 1980 and Menten, now 81 and with his mental health in question, objected to his court-appointed lawyer and insisted on conducting his own defence. This time he developed a theme only hinted at in the earlier court case: to explain the many eyewitness identifications of him, he now contended that he had been confused with his younger brother, Dirk!

Dirk Menten, who lived in France and had long been estranged from his brother, replied by agreeing for the first time to give evidence against Pieter. In court, the two men came face to face for the first time in nearly 20 years. Dirk claimed that members of the family had become concerned after the war about Pieter's mental stability. As a precaution, they had drawn up a document in 1953 recording, among other things, that Pieter had told Dirk in 1943 that he had been present in Podhorodze at the time of the executions. The document did not specify Pieter's participation, but the prosecution contended that it was quite impossible for anyone to mistake him for Dirk.

On this occasion, the prosecution asked for a 20-year sentence and a fine of 100,000 guilders (over £20,000) to 'strike symbolically' at Menten's fortune. Menten was again found guilty of participation in the Podhorodze massacre. The court found it impossible to determine his exact role, but declared that, 'Between the members of this team there was such complete unanimity and co-operation that from the point of view of criminal law, it can be considered unimportant which of them shot the victims. All members of the team must therefore be considered culprits.'

The fine demanded by the prosecution was granted, and Menten was jailed for ten years. He was freed after serving a third of his sentence.

CHAPTER 7

Historic Precedents

Adolf Beck
William Palmer
Palimony

Daniel M'Naghten
W.T. Stead

Mistaken identity

ADOLF BECK

Suppose it happened to you. Suppose that while walking down the street one day you were mistaken for the author of a theft, or a rape, or a murder? Suppose you were tried and convicted? Perhaps everyone has had their own dark thoughts about such possibilities. Today, the law provides certain safeguards against wrongful arrest and conviction, but it has not always been so.

The Court of Criminal Appeal was created by a statute of 1907. Before then, there was practically no way in which a convicted person could appeal against a miscarriage of justice. And though many eminent reformers help to shape the institution, society's thanks really belong to a hapless individual named Adolf Beck.

Born in Norway in 1841, Beck had lived a cosmopolitan life in South America and England. One day in 1895, as he was walking down Victoria Street near London's Army and Navy Stores, an enraged German lady named Ottilie Meissonier accosted him with demands that he give back her watches and rings.

Watches? Rings? Beck did not know what she was talking about, and when she persisted he ran off to tell a policeman that a strange lady was annoying him. She in turn complained that he had stolen her valuables. Together they went to Rochester Row police station, and there Adolf Beck's martyrdom began.

Ottilie Meissonier, who was a language teacher, informed the police that a month beforehand, in the same street, a man had greeted her on the pavement as Lady Everton. Although she explained his mistake, they engaged in conversation and he seemed very charming. She invited him home, where he described himself as a cousin of Lord Salisbury, then prime minister, and spoke of vast country estates. He invited her to join him on a yacht trip to the Riviera, wrote her a cheque to buy a suitable wardrobe for the voyage and — by a clever ruse — persuaded her to part with her rings and two wristwatches.

Of course, he turned out to have been a confidence trickster. The cheque was worthless. But luckily she spotted the man working the same patch at Victoria: and here he was — Adolf Beck — there could be no mistake about it at all.

It transpired that a number of women had been rooked by the confidence trickster in much the same way, and an identity parade was assembled in which each of the victims positively identified Beck. Furthermore, two policemen described how they had arrested just such a fraud several years earlier. He had been tried and convicted in 1877 under the name of 'John Smith', and they said that Beck was the man.

Adolf Beck was tried at the Old Bailey. The only real evidence against him was that of eyewitness identification, and there were disturbing irregularities in procedure. Beck could show he was not John Smith, for he had been in South America from 1873–84 while Smith was serving his five-year sentence. Moreover, their handwriting samples differed. But the judge ruled that the John Smith case should not be reopened in court, and that proved damning for Beck. Convicted on 5 March 1896, he was sentenced to seven years of penal servitude.

In prison, the authorities treated Beck exactly as if he were Smith, even giving him the former convict's prison number. All his protests availed nothing — even when the records disclosed that John Smith had been circumcized and he was not!

Beck served five years of his sentence and was released on licence in 1901. He may have thought then that his troubles were over. But only three years later a new series of confidence tricks was played on ladies in London. The police's thoughts turned to Beck and he was once more hauled up in the Old Bailey. The trial took place in June 1904, and again all the women witnesses identified Beck as the villain. Again he was found guilty. But this time, a more responsible judge delayed passing sentence — and at last daylight broke on the case.

The police disclosed that they had arrested a man who they believed was the real confidence trickster. He was operating under the name of

William Thomas, but his thefts bore all the hallmarks of the man whose career they had been following. He was much the same height and build as Adolf Beck; he had the same hairstyle, moustaches and head-shape. The two men, in fact, bore a marked resemblance (although they were by no means identical). When brought to trial, William Thomas pleaded guilty to the several charges against him — he also admitted that he was the man imprisoned in 1877 under the name of John Smith.

William Thomas, alias John Smith, was duly tried, convicted and sentenced. It was now clear to everyone that a terrible wrong had been done to Adolf Beck: he was freed, pardoned and awarded £5,000 compensation for the years he had spent in prison.

It would have made a neater story, perhaps, if he had lived to a ripe old age as a pillar of the community. In fact, Beck blew all his compensation money in a wild spending spree and died destitute only five years later. But his case lived on in the annals of the law as a classic of mistaken identity. The Beck affair shamed society into creating the Court of Appeal, which reformers had long been calling for. And it concentrated minds wonderfully on the issue of identity parades. In future, juries would be directed not to place absolute faith in identification. The eyes can deceive, and no-one would be safe strolling down a street if their evidence was regarded as infallible. Suppose, after all, that it happened to you. . . .

Mad or bad?

DANIEL M'NAGHTEN

In 1843, a Scotsman named Daniel M'Naghten shot and killed the prime minister's secretary, Edward Drummond, thinking that he was the premier, Robert Peel. The outrage occurred in a London street, and it was soon found that M'Naghten suffered from delusions. He thought he was being persecuted by the Tories of Glasgow, his native city, and gave a rambling statement to the examining magistrate. He said that his persecutors followed him everywhere — to France, to Scotland, all over England — and that he got no rest from them day or night. They had ruined his health, and had 'accused me of crimes of which I am not guilty. They do everything in their power to harass and persecute me. In fact they wish to murder me. It can be proved by evidence. . . .'

Fingers of Fate

Petty criminals Alfred and Albert Stratton made British legal history through their trial in May 1905. The brothers were the first people ever convicted of murder by the evidence of fingerprints.

In the course of a housebreaking, the Strattons had killed an elderly Deptford shopkeeper and his wife. Alfred had left a clear thumbprint on a rifled cashbox, and it was produced in evidence at the Old Bailey. In a fiercely contested forensic battle, a defence expert pointed to certain discrepancies between Stratton's print and that found on the box. But the prosecution replied that these were only minor differences resulting from the thumb pressures applied. The point was dramatically illustrated when jury members themselves had their prints repeatedly taken, and discovered similar discrepancies.

The jury was won over. Despite a cautious summing up from the judge on the value of fingerprint evidence, the Strattons were found guilty. They hanged together.

Of course, the phantom legions of enemies were all in M'Naghten's mind. The prisoner was mad — suffered from a persecution mania — as ample evidence was to demonstrate. And when his trial for murder came up in March 1843 the judge stopped the case, directing the jury to find a verdict of Not Guilty on grounds of insanity.

Nevertheless, the case had unfolded at a time of some political unrest when people had reason to fear terrorist conspiracy. There was much public concern over M'Naghten's acquittal, and the House of Lords took the unusual step of questioning the judges of England on the subject of insanity and the law. They put five questions in all, and the judges' answers became known as the M'Naghten Rules — an authority by which a defence of insanity could be tested. The Rules have since been applied throughout most of the English-speaking world, including the United States. Time and again they have been hotly debated when prisoners have appeared to occupy the shadowy zone on the frontiers of madness and badness.

The key passage in the rules declares that, to establish a defence of insanity, it must be clearly proved that, at the time of the crime, the accused was suffering 'such a defect of reason, from disease of mind, as not to know the nature and quality of the act he was doing; or if he did know it, that he did not know he was doing what was wrong'.

The rule poses two awkward problems: first, a 'disease of the mind' is not so easy to diagnose as measles. Second, the rule places great emphasis on 'knowing' an act to be wrong. Yet some people who are plainly mad may *know* their acts are wrong but do them compulsively, driven by their sickness. Madness can make you lose control rather than lose understanding.

The rules have been severely tested over the years. Following the case of Ronald True (see page 12), for example, a committee was set up to report on the issue, but the rules survived intact. In England, a concession to loss of control is enshrined in Section 2 of the Homicide Act. Passed in 1957, it provides for a defence of diminished responsibility which was tested in, among other cases, the trial of the Yorkshire Ripper (see page 30).

The most curious thing about the M'Naghten Rules has been their longevity. They were never really intended to serve as a complete code but to answer for the case of one man. And Daniel M'Naghten should probably have been convicted under the M'Naghten Rules: after all, it is fair to assume that he knew he was committing murder, and that murder is wrong.

Victorian villainies of the demon Doctor WILLIAM PALMER

A curious affliction struck those close to Dr Palmer of Rugeley — the affliction of sudden death. His mother-in-law; his wife; his brother; his illegitimate children; assorted creditors . . . altogether some 14 people are reckoned to have perished at the good doctor's hands. His were villainies accomplished in the grand manner, seeming to belong less to the humdrum routines of everyday life than to some stage-set Victorian melodrama.

William Palmer qualified as a doctor at St Bartholomew's Hospital and set up practice at Rugeley, Staffordshire, in 1846. A lover of the good life and of the turf, he came to own his own stable and several racecourses. But he lacked the income to support his expensive habits, and his financial problems sparked his career of crime. Palmer's mother-in-law, for example, died so that he could inherit her fortune. He poisoned his wife and brother shortly after having them heavily insured. The illegitimate children, of course, were an inconvenience; then there was the friend to whom he owed £800. Incredibly, no-one seems to have suspected Dr Palmer until 1855, when his friend John Parsons Cook suddenly took ill at a supper party. He and Palmer had been to the Shrewsbury Races together and Cook won handsomely while Palmer — in debt as ever — had lost. At supper, when Cook fell sick, it was Palmer who collected his winnings (using them to fend off his creditors). And later, when Cook retired to his death bed, it was Palmer who ministered to him.

A local physician diagnosed apoplexy, but the victim's relatives were suspicious and an autopsy conducted by the eminent toxicologist Dr Alfred Taylor showed the presence of the poison antimony in the organs. The inquest turned in a verdict of wilful murder and Palmer was put under arrest.

Under normal circumstances, Dr Palmer would have been tried by an Assize Court in Staffordshire. But the feeling against him was so strong in his native county that exceptional measures were required to guarantee him a fair trial. So a special Act was passed by Parliament, permitting the proceedings to take place at the Central Criminal Court in London. The historic 'Palmer Act', as it came to be known, subsequently provided any accused person facing similar local hostility the opportunity of a London trial.

Palmer was brought before an Old Bailey jury on 14 May 1856. Aged 32, he was charged solely that he 'feloniously, wilfully and with malice aforethought committed murder on the person of John Parsons Cook'. But though he was not indicted for any of the earlier crimes suspected of him, he would if acquitted face immediate trial for the murder of his wife and brother.

In fact, the Cook trial revealed a whole sorry saga of debts and forgeries, but the murder turned out to be exceptionally hard to prove. Everything hinged on complex medical testimony given on the nature of the poison used. Symptoms of the victim's death strongly suggested strychnine, but only antimony was present in the organs. It is thought that Palmer must have used his medical knowledge to seek out some related but less easily traced substance than strychnine, and his own words are interesting in this context. Palmer never confessed to his guilt; but he reiterated a carefully phrased claim that he was 'innocent of poisoning Cook by strychnia'. It did not follow, of course, that he was innocent of poisoning his friend by other means.

Tried and found guilty, he met his end with cool composure. On the morning of 14 June 1856 he was led out to the gallows before Stafford Gaol; it had rained and Dr Palmer is said to have 'minced along like a delicate schoolgirl, picking his way and avoiding the puddles'. A vast multitude comprising perhaps 50,000 people had come to witness the hanging and they greeted him with 'a deafening round of shouts, oaths and execrations' as he mounted the scaffold. The historic Act which bore his name only provided for trial in London. No-one thought it was strange that he should be conveyed back to Staffordshire for the grand spectacle of his public execution.

White slavery in London W. T. STEAD

When the doomed luxury liner *Titanic* struck an iceberg and sank on 15 April 1912, 1,513 people died. Among those who perished with the ship was William Thomas Stead, a journalist and newspaper editor well known for his writings on spiritualism, on the peace movement and other themes. But Stead was still remembered above all for a sensational press campaign which he had led almost 30 years before. It had invited comfortable middle-class readers to explore the moral sewers of Victorian London, exposing the practices of white slavery and child prostitution almost commonplace in the nation's capital. And it had changed the law of the land.

It was a deliberate attempt to change the law, too. Early in 1885, W. T. Stead was privately approached by supporters of the Criminal Law Amendment Bill, which, it was hoped, would help put an end to child prostitution in London. At that time, the age of consent to sexual intercourse was only 13. A girl barely at puberty could be enticed into a brothel and violated without fear of legal redress as long as the seducer could show that she entered the house freely. What happened to her afterwards was held to be at her own wish.

The Criminal Law Amendment Bill provided, among other things, for the raising of the age of consent to 16; it also allowed the issue of search warrants where it was suspected that any woman was being unlawfully detained for immoral purposes. All very sensible and humane, you might think; but the Bill had many opponents. For one thing, it proposed immunity to prostitutes testifying against their clients, and this seemed to offer a blackmailer's charter (indeed, Oscar Wilde was to be prosecuted under its provisions).

In all events, the Bill had been put before Parliament many times, and many times it was defeated. W. T. Stead was approached as a campaigning journalist who alone might give its cause the necessary publicity. And when the plight of seduced girls was explained to him fully he determined to 'raise hell' so that their cries could be heard.

Born in 1849, Stead was a kindly man with a curious mixture of puritanism and journalistic flair in his character. The son of a Congregational minister, he had joined the staff of the daily *Pall Mall Gazette* at 31, and by 1883 had become its editor. In that capacity he proved a brilliant innovator, introducing among other things the newspaper interview of celebrities. And his crusade on behalf of the child prostitutes of London showed him to be a pioneer of investigative journalism.

To show how easy it was to 'buy' a 13-year-old, he decided to pose as a roué and go through all the motions of forced seduction, stopping short only at the final act. (In terms later made famous by the *News of the World*, he would at the critical moment 'make an excuse and leave'.) To find a suitable girl, he called on the services of the Salvation Army, and in particular of a Salvationist named Rebecca Jarrett, who had once been a brothel-keeper. Her job would be to make contact with a destitute family willing to sell their daughter for immoral purposes.

Rebecca Jarrett, a reformed character, baulked at the idea at first. But eventually she was persuaded to collaborate in the scheme and came up with a Marylebone family named Armstrong. The father was a chimney sweep and the mother, according to Rebecca Jarrett, was willing to hand over their daughter Eliza in return for a mere £3.

The deal was done. Little Eliza was delivered into Stead's hands and, posing as her would-be debaucher, he drugged her with chloroform and took her to a house of ill fame run by a disreputable Frenchwoman, Mme Louise Mourey. The 'Madame' conducted an examination of the girl, who was then taken to bed. Having spent some time drinking champagne with the brothel-keeper, Stead entered little Eliza's room.

The girl woke up in fright; Stead 'made his excuse and left'; Eliza was drugged again and conveyed to a nursing home, where it was formally certified that she had suffered no physical injury. Eventually, she was whisked across the Channel and kept for safety at the Salvation Army centre in Paris.

It had all been accomplished with sinister ease; little Eliza might have been seduced and sold into slavery almost anywhere in the world. And armed with his material Stead was now ready to start the campaign. Over two weeks in July he ran Eliza's story in the *Pall Mall Gazette* under the heading 'The Maiden Tribute of Modern Babylon'.

The Law West of the Pecos

Among the legendary judges of the past was whiskery, whisky-sodden Roy Bean, whose Texas saloon at Langtry comprised the 'Law West of the Pecos' for two decades. He often stopped trials to serve liquor to the court, and once discharged one of his regulars (accused of murdering a Mexican) on the grounds that 'it served the deceased right for getting in front of a gun'. Thumbing through his battered Texas Statutes, he discharged another (accused of murdering a Chinese workman) on the grounds that 'there ain't a damn line here nowheres that makes it illegal to kill a Chinaman'.

The Judge also did funerals and weddings. He once fined a corpse $40 for carrying a concealed weapon, and always concluded marriage ceremonies with the words, 'May God have mercy on your soul.'

The details, of course, were authentic; but Stead omitted to inform his readers that he himself was the 'roué' and the girl had come to no harm. Instead, he posed it as a real-life tragedy — fully documented — of the modern age.

It was the great journalistic shocker of the era. The articles caused a furore, and editions of the *Gazette* sold out as soon as they were printed — despite the fact that W. H. Smith banned the offending issues from its station bookstalls. Nor were newsagents alone in deeming the articles obscene. Angry mobs laid siege to the newspaper's offices in Northumberland Street and police cordons were brought in to protect the premises. (It was not always clear what the mob wanted though — a hooligan element appeared to be clamouring for copies of the latest issues which had sold out everywhere else.) In Parliament, the Home Secretary was asked whether Stead could not be prosecuted for publishing such filth.

At the root of it all was hypocrisy — the arch hypocrisy of a prudish morality that forbade mention of sex while permitting prostitutes to choke London's streets in numbers estimated at some 100,000. Stead had raised hell all right — the hell of the Victorian underworld and all its degraded womanhood.

But his crusade did not quite go as planned. Mrs Armstrong, reviled by her neighbours as the callous mother of the articles, protested that the charges were untrue: she had never sold her daughter as alleged, and she demanded that the police try to find her daughter. Stead then disclosed that Eliza had come to no harm, and that he had been the pretended 'debaucher'. The confession led with fateful logic to his own prosecution for abduction, along with his various collaborators: Sampson Jacques (an assistant); Bramwell Booth of the Salvation Army; Rebecca Jarrett; and Louise Mourey.

The sensational trial opened at the Old Bailey on 23 October 1885, and it lasted until 10 November. Stead insisted on conducting his own defence, but his cause was poorly served by the testimony of a very miserable Rebecca Jarrett. It became obvious as the trial progressed that she had badly misled the newspaper editor about the initiation of the transaction.

For one thing, Rebecca Jarrett had never told Mrs Armstrong that her daughter was to be sold into prostitution as Stead believed; on the contrary, realizing that Mrs Armstrong would not part with Eliza on those terms, she had invented a story about the girl being taken into domestic service. Moreover, Stead had always thought that the father had consented to the deal; this, it seemed was not true. Nor could Stead substantiate the claims made in his articles that the sweep was a drunken brute. The Attorney General rapped his knuckles sharply on this point with the remark, 'I have yet to learn that a man with black hands has of necessity a black heart.'

In vain did Stead address the jury with an impassioned appeal for the wretched girls — 'as innocent as any of your daughters' — of the metropolis. The fact was that in the case of Eliza Armstrong a girl had been taken from her parents by deceit and made the subject of a journalistic experiment. On a point of law, the judge ruled that the father's consent must be proved if a charge of abduction was to be avoided. That consent had never been given.

The jury had no alternative but to return a verdict of guilty. However, they did so with a strong recommendation to mercy in Stead's case. The judge did little to conceal his distaste for the whole affair, and reproached Stead in the most severe terms: 'I regret to say that you have thought fit to publish in the *Pall Mall Gazette* a distorted account of the case of Eliza Armstrong, and that you deluged for some months our streets and the whole country with an amount of filth which I fear tainted the minds of the children you were so anxious to protect.'

Describing the campaign as 'a disgrace to journalism', the judge sentenced W. T. Stead to three months' imprisonment. Sampson Jacques got one month; Bramwell Booth was acquitted; Rebecca Jarrett got six months and Louise Mourey six months with hard labour.

Stead served his sentence in gaol, reflecting no doubt on his mixed fortunes. He had lost in court, but his crusade had by no means failed. The Criminal Law Amendment Act had been rushed through Parliament as a direct result of his articles — it was in force at the beginning of 1886, before he had even left prison.

Palimony — two famous cases

LEE MARVIN, BILLIE JEAN KING

It all started in 1979, when film star Lee Marvin was sued by his former mistress, Michelle Triolo Marvin. The pair had long lived together as lovers but, like so many laid-back couples on the West Coast they had never bothered to get married. This created no problems so long as the relationship held. But what when it broke down? Why should not Michelle expect the same rights of property as a divorced wife? After all, the two of them had cohabited for some six years — substantially longer than many conventionally married couples.

That was Michelle's thinking, and in April 1979 she won what seemed to be a major test case for all women in California — and throughout the United States. After a much-publicized trial, in which

Hollywood star, Lee Marvin

the film star's private life was explored with glee by reporters, the Californian Supreme Court ruled that, on principle, unmarried people who live together could have contractual property rights similar to those of married couples. Michelle argued that, though nothing had been put into writing, an implied contract did exist, and she was awarded $104,000. The sum was not for breach of contract but 'damages', as it were, for the years they had lived together; something to enable her to start a new life.

Lee Marvin, however, took his case to California's Appeal Court, which in August 1981 set aside the award. It was ruled that the film star need not pay the money, on the grounds that his former girlfriend had not proved that damages were sustained as a result of living with him. Eventually, in January 1982, Michelle finally gave up any attempt to obtain the money. Her cause had ended in defeat.

Nevertheless, the Supreme Court's original ruling had encouraged dozens of other Californians, separated from their lovers, to seek property settlements as if they had been married. The term 'palimony' was coined to describe the settlements, and the most sensational case revolved around tennis star Billie Jean King.

Mrs King had been married for 16 years to sports promoter Larry King. Yet in April 1981, an astonished public learned that she was to be sued by her former secretary — a woman — who alleged that she and Mrs King had lived together for many years in a lesbian relationship. There had never yet been a homosexual palimony case, and the issue could hardly have found a more famous protagonist than the six-times Wimbledon singles champion.

Marilyn Barnett, 33, a one-time hairdresser, had filed a 13-page suit seeking lifetime support and title to a beach house in Malibu which she claimed that Mrs King had promised her. She claimed that in or about May 1972 she and Mrs King met and began dating on a regular basis. Sexual intimacy had begun some six months after the first date and Ms Barnett claimed that she gave up her hairdressing career to become Billie Jean's secretary, abandoning 'all other things so that King's energy could be totally directed towards tennis'. In 1979, Ms Barnett claimed, Mrs King breached an oral contract by demanding that she move out of the Malibu house so that it could be sold.

Some months before the suit was filed, Marilyn Barnett had fallen from the balcony of a building; she was now a paraplegic.

Initially, Mrs King was reported to have denied the homosexual relationship, saying, 'I am completely shocked and disappointed by the action Miss Barnett has taken.' She added that the woman had indeed worked as her secretary in the 1970s, but had been 'phased out' when Mrs King started to reduce her business activities in order to concentrate on tennis.

The next day, however, the tennis star called a press conference in Los Angeles and, against the advice of her lawyers, admitted, 'I did have an affair with Marilyn Barnett.'

Billie Jean's husband and parents were at the conference and gave her full support as she addressed the journalists. 'I've always been honest,' she said, 'I've decided to talk with you as I've always talked — from my heart.' Of her former lover, she said, 'I am very disap-

Marilyn Barnett, one time lover of Billie Jean

pointed and shocked that Marilyn has done this, not only to herself —
a very self-destructive thing — but to other people who care for her.'
Though the affair had been over for some time, she admitted, 'I made
a mistake. I will assume that responsibility. I discussed it with Larry
— in some ways I think we're much closer today than we've ever been,
and our marriage is stronger.'

As for Ms Barnett's property claims, Mrs King denied the promise
of lifetime support, the beach house or any other financial arrange-
ment. And she declined to comment on press stories that Marilyn
Barnett had become a paraplegic in a suicide leap — rather than fall
— from a balcony.

Not long afterwards, Mrs King tendered her resignation as president
of the Women's Tennis Association. That resignation was rejected by
WTA authorities, and in general the public response was overwhelm-
ingly favourable toward the beleaguered tennis star. Letters and tele-
grams of support came to her by the sackful, and sympathy only
increased when it was alleged that a national tabloid was offering
$25,000 for some 100 love letters written by her to her former secretary.
(Those letters were not, in fact, to be publicized; lawyers acting for
the two women made a joint agreement to keep their contents secret.)

When the case came to court, it came in two parts. The first suit, heard in December 1981, was in fact brought by Mrs King and her husband to force Marilyn Barnett to leave their beach home. The former hairdresser hobbled with a walking stick into the Superior Court at Los Angeles, wearing a long grey skirt to hide her leg braces. In the witness stand she was asked by Mrs King's counsel what she had done for his client.

'I gave up my career, my identity, my pride and my home,' replied Ms Barnett. She said that she had hoped her relationship with Billie Jean would last for life and, asked if she felt that the tennis star owed her something, she replied firmly, 'Yes.'

Nobody could deny that a deep human drama underlay the court-room wranglings. But Mrs King, who watched arm in arm with her husband, was granted the decision, winning the right to evict her former lover from the disputed beach house. The judge had ruled that Ms Barnett had come close to trying to extort money from the tennis star; it appeared that Billie Jean and her husband had offered her $125,000 to get her to leave the house. Ms Barnett had refused, according to the judge, because she felt that she could get more money.

Almost a year later, in November 1982, a judge dismissed Marilyn Barnett's remaining claims. Like the Marvin case, the suit had created immense public interest and helped to cement an important legal principle. But in practice, a plea for palimony had failed again.

Billie Jean King with husband Larry

Acknowledgements

A book of this nature must inevitably draw on existing published material. In recent cases, the author has made use of trial reports in *The Times*, *The Guardian*, *The Sunday Times*, and *The Observer*. Additionally, the author wishes to acknowledge his debt to the following books:

Famous Trials, selected by John Mortimer, Penguin Books, 1984
Famous and Infamous Cases, Patrick Hastings KC, Heinemann 1950
Crime and Detection, an Illustrated History, Julian Symons, Studio Vista, 1966
Cases that Changed the Law, H. Montgomery Hyde, Heinemann, 1951
The Murderers' Who's Who, Gaute and Odell, Harrap, 1979
The Poisoned Life of Mrs Maybrick, Bernard Ryan, Kimber, 1977
Raymond Chandler Speaking, Ed. Dorothy Gardiner and Kathrine Walker, Hamish Hamilton, 1962
Sir Walter Raleigh, Willard M. Wallace, O.U.P., 1959
More Famous Trials, The Earl of Birkenhead, Hutchinson, 1938
State Crimes, Horace King, Dent, 1967
Deacon Brodie, Father to Jekyll and Hyde, John S. Gibson, Paul Harris, 1977
Crimes of Passion, Treasure Press, 1983
Encyclopaedia of Espionage, Ronald Seth, New English Library, 1972
Operation Overflight, Francis Gary Powers, Hodder and Stoughton, 1971
Nuremberg, a Nation on Trial, Werner Maser, Allen Lane, 1979
The Nuremberg Trial, Ann Tusa and John Tusa, Macmillan, 1983
Justice in Jerusalem, Gideon Hausner, Nelson, 1966
Public Scandal, Odium and Contempt, David Hooper, Secker and Warburg, 1984
The Menten Affair, Hans Knoop, Robson Books, 1979
The DeLorean Tapes, Sunday Times insight, Collins, 1984
Sixty Famous Trials, Ed. Richard Huson, Daily Express, 1938
Lost Causes, James Comyn, Secker and Warburg, 1982
Notable Cross Examinations, Edward Fordham, Constable, 1951
The Thalidomide Children and the Law, Sunday Times, André Deutsch, 1973
Guilty But Insane, G. W. Keeton, Macdonald, 1961
Murder 'Whatdunit', Gaute and Odell, Harrap, 1982
The Trial of Marie Stopes, Ed. Muriel Box, Femina, 1967
The Trial of Stephen Ward, Ludovic Kennedy, Gollancz, 1964
The Trial of Lady Chatterley, Ed. C. H. Rolph, Private printing, 1961
Notable British Trials Series (*Oscar Wilde, H. H. Crippen, William Palmer, Ronald True*) William Hodge

The publishers would like to thank the following for their kind permission to reproduce the pictures used in this book:
Topham Picture Library except for pages 2 below left, 35, 91, 127 which were supplied by The Photo Source